ASK
ME
ANYTHING

ASK ME ANYTHING

Annie Lane

with Courtney Davison

Creators Publishing

Hermosa Beach, CA

ASK ME ANYTHING

Cover design by Courtney Davison

CREATORS PUBLISHING
737 3rd St
Hermosa Beach, CA 90254
310-337-7003

This book is not intended as a substitute for the medical advice of physicians or psychiatrists. The reader should consult a physician in matters relating to his or her health, particularly with respect to any symptoms that may require diagnosis or medical attention. The authors have made every effort to ensure the accuracy of the information within this book was correct at time of publication. The authors do not assume and hereby disclaims any liability to any party for any loss, damage, or disruption caused by errors or omissions, whether such errors or omissions result from accident, negligence, or any other cause.

Library of Congress Control Number: 2017962926
ISBN (print): 9781945630781
ISBN (ebook): 9781945630767

First Edition
Printed in the United States of America
1 3 5 7 9 10 8 6 4 2

To everyone who has written to me.
You make this column possible.

Contents

Etiquette, Etc.

◆

Family

Friendship

◆

Love

◆

Author's Note

No matter how convinced you are that a letter
is about your family, any similarity to any person or
situation is purely coincidental. Names, jobs, genders, ages and
other identifying details have all been changed.
These are opinions, and they're meant
for entertainment purposes, first and foremost.
If you are having a medical emergency, or feel that you are a
danger to yourself or others, please call 911.
Asking for help is a sign of strength, not weakness.
A list of resources is available at the back of this book.

—Annie Lane

HOW DO I TELL MY BUDDY HE SMELLS LIKE A BARNYARD ANIMAL?

Etiquette, Etc.

Don't Pet My Puppy

DEAR ANNIE: My puppy, a beagle/Labrador mix, is 1 year old and does everything puppies do. She's adorbs. She's a traffic-stopper. My heart melts when I see her. But she also does her business in the house, chews on everything and has seemingly endless amounts energy. She is still in training and will be in training for another year—at least.

One of the things we're working on is getting her to stop jumping up on people. If she starts to jump, I'm supposed to turn around and ignore her until she stops. I do this at home, and it works well.

But whenever I take her for walks, strangers see what a cutie she is and want to pet her. When they approach her and she jumps, they say that typical phrase I've come to hate: "Oh, it's OK. I don't mind." I get so frustrated with these people. I find myself snapping back at them, "But I do!" I am having trouble being patient with every single person who does this, because I feel as though every time it happens, it ruins the progress of my pup's training. I don't know what to say to strangers anymore.

—Puppy Parent

DEAR PUPPY: It's time for you to be the alpha dog. You must assert your dominance over your pup's interactions with strangers. The people who are doing this have obviously never had to train a dog before, so they're probably really confused when you snap at them—ostensibly just for petting your dog. Recognize the warning signs and stop the troublesome behavior before it starts.

The next time you see an approaching stranger giving your dog that oh-my-gosh-let-me-hug-you look, say, "You can pet her, but she's in training, so please don't let her jump. If she does, turn your back on her." You have to be proactive and take control of the situation early—like any good leader of the pack.

Hey, Where Are You?

DEAR ANNIE: I'm wondering whether you could settle a dispute between my friend "Laura" and me. She thinks it's rude to "ghost"—leave parties without saying bye. I think it's fine.

For example, last weekend, our mutual friend had a barbecue. This particular friend is a social butterfly, so there were probably close to 75 people there. I knew a dozen or so of the guests. I enjoyed catching up with them and meeting some new people, but after a couple of hours, my socializing meter was about up and I was ready to go home and get to bed.

I didn't want to take the trouble to say bye to everyone I knew there, so I just said good night to the people in my immediate vicinity and then stepped out quietly. About an hour later, Laura texted asking where I'd gone. When I told her I was already at home, she got angry and said it was rude for me not to say goodbye.

I really have never thought of it as rude. I think of it as a timesaver for everyone. I hate awkwardly interrupting the flow of conversations to tell people I'm leaving, especially because then other people usually chime in, "Oh, I should get going, too," and I feel as if I've killed the party. I just want to slip out quietly and let everyone else keep doing their thing.

What do you think, Annie? Is it bad manners to ghost?

—*Tiptoeing Toward the Exit*

DEAR TIPTOEING: People might better like your vanishing act if it came with a bang and a cloud of smoke. Almost all the people whom I've talked to about this maneuver say it drives them crazy. They'll be out with friends and suddenly have a "Home Alone"-like moment in which they realize they're one short.

Though I don't condone the behavior, I get it; you don't want to interrupt conversations or derail the party train. Plus, there's a frozen pizza at home calling your name. (Admit it.)

I think a good rule of thumb is: Don't ghost the host. You don't have to make the rounds to say bye to everyone you know, but at the very least, seek out the host to say thanks for having you. Then you may spirit yourself away and into some pajamas.

Can't Take It Nose More

DEAR ANNIE: Being the dutiful husband that I am, I drive my non-driving wife to work every day, and I pick her up after work. At her request, I also have been giving a lift home in the evenings to one of her co-workers. It's not far out of our way, and the fellow is pleasant and likable—well, with the exception that he smells like a farm animal and is totally oblivious to that fact.

It seems to me this man seldom bathes or changes his clothes. I drive with the windows open in the dead of winter, and in the summer, the odor is even more horrific. My wife acknowledges this issue but doesn't want to confront him or address it. I have no problem talking to this guy diplomatically and letting him know what's going on, but my wife has strongly asked me not to. So I suffer in silence.

How do I get out of this pickle without upsetting my wife or causing anyone any further embarrassment?

—*Need Oxygen*

DEAR OXYGEN: It's time to put this animal out to pasture. Your wife isn't considering the matter from your nose's perspective. It's nice enough you give them both rides; you shouldn't have to hold your breath the whole way. Tell your wife that either she needs to come up with a polite excuse for why you can't give this man rides anymore or you're going to have a frank discussion with him about personal hygiene. If she doesn't like it, they can both catch a lift on the hayride.

Blacking Out at College

DEAR ANNIE: I'm a 21-year-old college junior. I love college for every reason you would think.

I love the autonomy to select my own classes and study the things that interest me. I love the freedom to make my own schedule. I love being treated like an adult, in that nobody is making sure I go to class or do my schoolwork.

I also love college for the parties. Though I am by no means a lush, I go out and drink heavily Thursday, Friday and Saturday night almost every week. Most of those nights, I cannot remember chunks of the evening. I know that this might be jarring to hear, but it's the norm in college. The joke around campus is to ask your friends the next morning, "Did we see each other last night?"

I'm sure most doctors or alcohol treatment professionals would say that I (or a large percentage of American college kids) have a drinking problem, but it really doesn't feel that way. I have a cumulative 3.4 GPA, and I am telling you, everyone drinks and blacks out. It's not a big deal. So my question is: What's all the fuss about when it comes to blacking out? Isn't it just a rite of passage?

—*Fuzzy Student*

DEAR Fuzzy: Blacking out is not normal. Let me repeat: Blacking out is not normal. It might seem as if everyone is doing it, but people with drinking problems have a way of conveniently overestimating how much everyone else is drinking.

I would be willing to wager that your peers aren't blacking out so much as you think. If they are, you may be seeking out heavy drinkers to normalize your behavior.

6

I won't try to scare you out of drinking—mostly because that wouldn't work but also because drinking in moderation can be fine, if you can do it. So try it. Slow way down, and stop earlier. If you can't, then you have a problem. And the fact that you're writing to me indicates that on some level, you already know.

Are Business Cards a Thing of the Past?

DEAR ANNIE: While clearing out my desk and bookshelf for some late spring-cleaning, I came across a few business cards from folks I, at one time, thought I would definitely need or want to stay in contact with. But I haven't thought about them since their cards got lost in the shuffle. This got me thinking: How important or valuable are business cards these days?

In my experience as a young professional, there are two things I know for certain about how things are done these days: It's all about whom you know, and a lot of networking happens online, whether through LinkedIn or email. Don't get me wrong; I enjoy handing my card out to people I meet (especially a cute guy at a bar). It makes me feel confident and reputable. (Can you say "adulting"?) But is the move refreshing and old-school, or is it a waste of paper that will get stuck between a pile of receipts and valet stubs?

—*Clever or Never?*

DEAR CLEVER OR NEVER: In an age of all-digital everything, I find business cards refreshingly old-school.

They make a good impression that can help someone remember you even if he or she loses your card. And making an impression is what old-fashioned, technically-no-longer-necessary niceties are all about. It's why it's still advisable to send a handwritten thank-you note after a job interview even though you could just send an email. When you give out your card to people, just be sure to get their contact info, too, so you can follow up online.

Dozens of print companies now offer business cards that are recycled, recyclable, biodegradable—even seeded, meaning your new contact can bury the card in the yard and, in a few months, have tomatoes. Talk about a lasting impression.

Home Imposition

DEAR ANNIE: I'm getting sick of my living situation. After college, I moved in with a very close family friend. He has an awesome house right by the beach and was kind enough to offer me his spare bedroom for very cheap rent while I'm still looking for a full-time job. It was really perfect for the first few months; he's a really mellow, simple guy who generally keeps to himself. But lately, I feel as if I'm walking on eggshells at home.

You see, he's a bit older—in his 40s—and he has never been married. All of the furniture and appliances in the house are his. It's a pretty tiny space, so we agreed to just share appliances and things when I moved in. I've always been respectful of his space. At night, he likes to cook for hours and play video games in the living room until 11 o'clock or so.

8

Lately, if he comes home to me watching a movie on *his* TV or cooking on *his* stove or even just stretching before a workout in the living room, he gets all bunged up and passive-aggressive. I'm only comfortable when confined to my room. What's the best way to handle this?

—*Tiptoeing*

DEAR TIPTOEING: To think—a 40-something single man who prefers to be alone and play video games doesn't like sharing his space?! Shocking.

You have a right to feel comfortable, so talk to him and see what happens. It's unrealistic for him to expect you to live like a ghost. But at the end of the day, you are in *his* home, and this was supposed to be temporary. So enough with the tiptoeing. Pull yourself up by your bootstraps and march on to a new apartment.

Who's the One With the Bad Manners?

DEAR ANNIE: We have six children, all of whom are married and have children. All 33 of us get together at Christmas, with a specified time to start dinner. One daughter's family was late in 2015 and again in 2016. We did not wait for her to arrive before eating dinner, because everyone else was on time and hungry. When she arrived 45 minutes later with her family, she made the comment to her husband, "I told you my family has no manners. They wouldn't wait to start dinner."

Were we wrong to start without her group? I just want to do it right in 2017 without hurting any feelings. She lives only 20 minutes away, and yes, her children are young, but everyone else's children are also young, and they managed to arrive on time.

—*Waiting*

DEAR WAITING: I hope Santa brings her a watch this year, though it sounds as if she deserves coal. Your daughter, not you, is the one who needs to "do it right" in 2017. You were doing just fine. It would have been rude to ask the rest of your guests, who were hungry and ready to dig in, to sit and wait indefinitely. If your daughter doesn't like arriving when everyone is eating, she should try showing up on time. Tell her this (perhaps in slightly milder terms). Or tell her that the dinner starts 45 minutes before it actually does.

Bro, You Owe Me

DEAR ANNIE: Last year, I took my buddy "John" on an all-expenses-paid trip to Las Vegas. The trip was partly covered by my work, but I paid for an extra night so we could make a long weekend out of it. It was John's first time in Vegas, and he had beginner's luck, big-time. He ended up leaving with close to $2,000 more than he had when we got there. I didn't do so hot, but I digress.

The reason I'm writing to you is that John used the cash to buy tickets to a Cubs game—seventh row by first base—and I'm not invited. It's killing me. He's taking his wife, kids and in-laws. His wife hates sports and will probably be on her iPhone the whole time. His kids are 3 and 5, and there's no way they're going to sit still for three hours. I know that if I went, John would have a much better time. Plus, I feel that I played a part in getting him those tickets, seeing as I'm the one who invited him to Vegas and paid for everything in the first place.

What do you think? Do I have a leg to stand on here? How do I slyly invite myself along?

—*Go, Cubs*

DEAR GO: You don't.

John didn't realize that accepting your invitation for an expenses-paid trip to Vegas meant owing you a favor in return. That's not how giving works. If it's got strings attached, it's not a gift; it's a trap. Don't dare guilt him into giving you a ticket, unless a seat at one ballgame is worth more to you than your friendship (in which case, buy yourself some Cracker Jack and, please, never come back).

Crunchtime at Work

DEAR ANNIE: I am a 25-year-old woman working at a small company with an open floor plan in a nice, spacious office.

I sit near "Sarah," who seems irritable about a lot of things, including the sound of eating or drinking. Because of my fast metabolism and active lifestyle, I need to snack every hour or two.

At first, Sarah would put on her headphones, start blasting music and sigh loudly when I started eating—even if it was something quiet, such as a banana. She does the same when another co-worker drinks soda. When it became an obvious pattern, I privately asked a few co-workers (without mentioning Sarah) whether my frequent eating bothers them. They all told me it doesn't bother them. After all, we all snack at our desks, including Sarah.

Today Sarah got closer to being openly hostile, giving me a death stare every time I bit a carrot stick. I didn't react, but I'm starting to get uncomfortable. I would eat only on break and lunch if that were enough time, but it isn't.

Should I just ignore Sarah's hostile attitude toward me? Should I carefully ask her about what's bothering her or go through a supervisor? We don't have human resources.

—Girl Who's Gotta Eat

DEAR GIRL: The more time I spend writing about this sort of topic and hearing from readers, the more I realize there are two types of people in the world: those who can usually tune out background noise and those whose blood pressure starts rising the minute they hear someone opening a bag of chips. I'm guessing Sarah is in the latter camp.

The next time you start snacking and Sarah starts glaring, be direct. Ask her whether your eating is bothering her. Then explain what you told me—that you have a high metabolism and need to eat snacks throughout the day—and say you'd like to compromise and figure out a way for you to work near each other in harmony.

It's always better to clear the air—especially when you

consider how much carbon dioxide Sarah's letting out with all those exaggerated sighs.

You Gonna Need Change?

DEAR ANNIE: I have gotten to the point that I no longer like to go out to eat, especially if it is a restaurant that my wife and I have not gone to before. Here's why.

You have a great meal in a nice restaurant. The service was friendly and excellent. When the check comes and I put my money down for the waitress, she says as she picks it up, "Do you need change?"

This ticks me off to no end. I have, in the past, gone through the trouble to try to educate the servers, in the hope of breaking them of the habit. So I explain to them that you never, ever put the customer on the defensive by insinuating that he is cheap for wanting change from the bills he put down. The servers I explain this to sometimes understand, but most of the time, they do not. They just think I am some senior citizen who complains a lot.

I usually retaliate by leaving a small tip instead of the 20 to 25 percent that I would do otherwise. (I try to tip big because I know how little they make hourly.) Depending on how you and your readers look at it, I think I will leave a copy of my letter and your response along with the tip in the future.

—Frustrated in Maine

DEAR FRUSTRATED: True, it's not the best etiquette on a

server's part to ask whether you want change. But I think you're looking at this in the wrong light.

You're assuming that servers are insinuating you're cheap when they pose this question. I highly doubt that. Sure, there may be some servers out there who would use such tactics to try to shame a big tip out of customers. But most servers are more polite than that—and more intelligent. (Why risk offending someone precisely at the moment you want him to feel happiest with your service?) I find it more likely they're oblivious and just trying to save themselves a 30-second trip back to your table. In either scenario, a smile and a "yes, please" are the appropriate response.

But if I hear a convincing case against this, I'll print it here for you to clip and keep at the ready in your wallet.

An Acquaintance With No Boundaries

DEAR ANNIE: Morgan and I are from the same hometown, and a few weeks ago, she moved to the city where I live now. Though I'd never met her, we have a ton of mutual friends back home (or so I thought). She asked whether I'd show her around. I remembered what it was like to be new in town, so I was happy to help.

Morgan and I got along well and had a lot in common. The first night we went out, she asked whether she could sleep on my couch because it was so late. I said sure. Then she stayed the next night, without asking—and then the next. One morning, when I woke up, my car was gone. She had taken it to the store without even asking. She must have dug through my purse for the keys.

On top of this, she just got a job at the same store where I work. I started to get a little nervous about the lack of space, and I told her I needed to set some boundaries and hang out less.

This week, she asked whether she could live with me for a bit. I said no, but she won't stop bombarding me with calls. I asked a mutual friend what Morgan's deal is, and he told me that she's crazy and all our friends stopped talking to her years ago. Now what do I do? I feel really guilty ignoring her.

—Suffocating

DEAR SUFFOCATING: Run; don't walk. You set boundaries, and she disrespected them. You told her she couldn't live with you, and she wouldn't take no for an answer. All this and you've only known her for *three weeks*.

I'm sounding the stage-five "clinger" alarm. Stop letting this girl into your life. Don't feel guilty; don't entertain any sort of dialogue. If you give her an inch, she'll take a mile (along with your keys, wallet and Social Security number).

Tip Mortification

DEAR ANNIE: The other day, I was out for lunch with a woman I recently became friends with. At the end of the meal, we asked the server to split the check 50-50. He brought us our receipts. I was waiting for my friend to finish using the pen, and I wasn't trying to peek, but I noticed she'd left the tip line blank. She noticed my noticing and, only a little sheepishly, said, "I'm just not making that much money right now"—as if that were an acceptable reason to stiff our (very kind) server.

I was mortified but said nothing, took the pen and began writing in an extra-big tip to try to make up for her. She saw what I was doing and told me I shouldn't worry about it— that I was overreacting. I think she was being rude.

What do you think?

—*Tipped Off*

DEAR TIPPED OFF: Anyone who can't afford to leave a tip shouldn't be eating out in the first place. The next time this friend wants to get together, suggest something free— though, if you're the type of person who regards tipping as a sign of character (I do), you might not want to get together again at all.

Doing Business With Friends

DEAR ANNIE: I am a real estate agent in a wealthy part of Southern California. In my part of town, everyone knows everyone, especially in real estate.

I have my group of mom friends. Some of us work. Others do not. All of our kids go to the same school. We see one another multiple times every week.

My best friend in the group is a designer. She's relatively new to the real estate world, but she has a great eye for design. Another friend in the group is a financial adviser. She is a brilliant woman, so I hired her to manage my money, and I'm actually her Realtor.

I sold the money manager a house. I referred designer to money manager. Can you guess where this is going?

Long story short, money manager and designer had a huge falling out. Money manager claims she fired designer. Designer claims she walked off the job. Needless to say, they both think they are right.

I really don't care what happened between the two of them. I'm more concerned with my business. Was I stupid to refer designer to money manager? Should I find a different money manager so that we don't have a falling out?

I like doing business with friends because I trust them, but I don't want to lose any friends if business relationships go south.

—*Referral Referee*

DEAR REF: Good real estate agents, designers and financial advisers are a 10-second Yelp search away. Good friends, however, are a lot harder to find.

It's too late to repair the relationship between your two friends, but it's not too late for you to avoid a falling-out of your own. Hire a new person to manage your money. Explain to your friend it's precisely because you value your friendship that you want to stop doing business with her. If she's as smart as you say she is, she'll get it.

Eating Before the Host Sits

DEAR ANNIE: I am shocked when I am at a dinner party and see people eating before the hosts sit down with their meal. What if someone wants to make a toast or say a blessing before the meal? Is this the new normal in dining etiquette?

—Call Me Old-Fashioned

DEAR CALL: I'll only call you polite. Unless the host specifically insists otherwise (e.g., "Please, start eating before your food gets cold"), you should absolutely not begin eating until he or she is seated and there has been time to say grace. This gracious person took the time to prepare a beautiful meal to share with guests and shouldn't be treated like a waiter. So no, you're not old-fashioned. Good manners never go out of style.

Trespassing Neighbor

DEAR ANNIE: One of my home's attributes is that it has acres of conservation woods behind it. My neighbor from across the street, "Mr. X," has been crossing my property to dump his yard waste in the woods.

Today, I asked him to stop. The footing can be treacherous, and I don't want a lawsuit if Mr. X gets hurt. My property is not a right of way. Dumping on someone's land without permission is illegal in our state. I know he doesn't have permission.

I have no curtains on that side of the house and open my bathroom window all the way while I shower and dry off. It is creepy to look out my window and see someone who should not be there. I'm not hanging curtains. I shouldn't have to. He shouldn't be there.

When I informed Mr. X not to cross my property, he said he'd just go through another neighbor's yard to dump. He can still look right in. Contacting the owner of the conservation woods is not an option. I'm tempted to call in a peeping Tom report because it creeps me out so much. I want my privacy back. Any suggestions?

—*Creeped Out*

DEAR CREEPED: Who does this man think he is? He's awfully brazen. It sounds as if it's time for this little troll to be sent back under his bridge. Given that your neighborly chat accomplished nothing, I see no reason you shouldn't call your county's illegal-dumping hotline to report this crime. If you don't have such a hotline in your area, call the non-emergency number for the police. And in the meantime, it wouldn't hurt to get curtains.

Wading Through Messages

DEAR ANNIE: As of this writing, I have 6,972 unread emails.

A lot of them are promotions from stores I shopped at once. Some are from social media sites, telling me I have notifications—Facebook, LinkedIn, Pinterest—which I hardly ever check.

I guess I never got into the habit of deleting these messages as they came in, and then once the pile started growing, it just seemed so overwhelming that I gave up even trying. I wish I could just delete everything and start fresh, get my inbox back down to zero.

In some cases, I have emails from people I would like to talk to. For instance, my cousin, whom I haven't talked to in over a year, emailed me last month. I've kept putting it off until I have enough time to sit down and write a thoughtful response. Now it's been so long I feel awkward about replying.

I have a similar problem with voicemail. I delay checking my messages, and sometimes I just ignore them altogether.

After I click "send" on this email to you, I'm going to have anxiety about seeing your response. What is wrong with me? I feel paralyzed. How can I begin to tackle this?

—*Inbox Infinity*

DEAR INBOX: Procrastination and anxiety are each other's best cheerleader. Anxiety encourages procrastination, and vice versa. Remove one of them and you'll deflate the other.

So start by calming down. Tell yourself, "Nothing catastrophic is going to happen because I didn't delete emails." Although such a laissez-faire attitude might seem counterproductive, it's a lot easier to get moving once you take that enormous weight off your shoulders.

Then snap to it and get that inbox under control, first by

plugging the dam so you can prevent floods of promotional emails in the future. Open the latest email you received, and scroll to the bottom. Look for the "unsubscribe" button (in microscopic font). Do that for every major vendor that's flooding your inbox.

Next, delete with abandon. Trash every promotional email that's more than a week old. Resist the urge to save emails "just in case." If you were really interested in reading last week's Pinterest newsletter, you already would have.

Wedding Guests Left Hanging

DEAR ANNIE: I recently attended a couple of weddings that left me baffled.

The custom of most weddings in the Midwest is for the wedding couple and their wedding party to hire a limo, party bus or some other method of transportation to take the whole group around to various bars after the wedding ceremony and before the reception, usually held at another establishment. The guests are free to go to the reception site, and usually some type of refreshment is offered.

At one particular wedding, the couple did not even greet their guests at the back of the church after the ceremony. They secluded themselves in another room and left their parents to greet and thank the guests for coming, and then they made their exit from the church with the usual fanfare and entered the party bus. It was more than two hours before they made an entrance at the reception. Meanwhile, the guests were left waiting for the couple to arrive before they were offered the reception meal. Some guests were elderly or had traveled a long distance and wanted to go home after the reception, so after two hours, they left without waiting for the couple.

Since another recent wedding, the bride has been selling unwanted gifts on the Facebook Marketplace forum. Are we wrong to feel that our gifts were not appreciated? Perhaps this is easier than returning unwanted items to the store, or maybe the couple only really wanted money, but with far-reaching social media, I am sure some guests are seeing their gifts being sold within a month of the wedding and before the thank-you cards are even sent.

I realize that the happy couple would like to celebrate with their friends, but shouldn't consideration for their guests come first? At least make an appearance early at the reception so that the guests can enjoy that time, as well. And for goodness' sake, have the grace to appreciate the time and effort guests have put into their gifts

—Wedding Blues

DEAR WEDDING BLUES: Selling wedding gifts on social media is tacky, plain and simple. I'd never heard of that before, and I hope to never hear of it again. Newlyweds, if you don't want a gift, just return it.

As for the hourslong wait for the couple to make their entrance at the reception, I've noticed this trend. I believe it's because photographers can take more photos now than ever, and photo shoots are elaborate, with multiple locations and every possible combination of wedding party members.

I encourage anyone planning a wedding to take guests' needs into account. If there is going to be significant lag between the ceremony and the reception, make sure guests have somewhere to socialize and something to eat.

Family Member Won't Pay for Damage

DEAR ANNIE: I am finding myself in a predicament. Currently, my sister-in-law baby-sits my 3- and 5-year-old children two days a week while I am at work. Last week, when I went to pick them up, I parked behind her fiancé's truck. Her fiancé, "Brad," was getting ready to leave at the same time I was. Instead of waiting for me to move from behind his vehicle, he squeezed around my car between other vehicles in the driveway. When I got home, I noticed that his tire had rubbed against my car and put several scratches in the paint.

Well, I called my sister-in-law, as I don't know Brad very well, and explained to her what had happened. I said I think Brad needs to pay for damages. She said she doesn't want to be in the middle of things and would give him my number.

Several days went by, and I didn't hear from Brad. In the meantime, I got an estimate for repairs. I talked to my sister-in-law again, and she said she would have Brad call me. Well, he finally did that evening, and he gave me about a dozen different scenarios of how he thinks the situation might have happened, but he said that there is no way he did it and that he isn't paying for it. I am sure he hit my car, and I told him that. He told me he had gone to my workplace to look at my vehicle and gone to the body shop and asked to see pictures of the damage. I thought that was disturbing. The conversation ended with him swearing at me and hanging up. The next day, Brad called my husband to also tell him he isn't paying and offered no apologies for his behavior.

The problem I now have is how to handle the baby-sitting situation. Brad lives at my sister-in-law's home, and I really don't want to have any more confrontations with him. My sister-in-law loves my children and would be heartbroken if I got a different sitter. But I really don't think I am comfortable taking them to her house with Brad around.

Should I follow my gut feeling and stop taking them there and further divide my family's relationship? Or should I try to get past the vehicle damage? I am also worried about how any possible repercussions against me by Brad would affect my children. How do you think I should proceed from here?

—*Scuffed*

DEAR SCUFFED: The answer to the question "Should I follow my gut?" is always yes. And if you're a mom, the answer is yes with three exclamation points. A mother's intuition is a tool more reliable and precious than any piece of technology.

So if you feel uncomfortable leaving your children around this man, then don't. Invite your sister-in-law over for coffee so she can still visit with the kids. Given Brad's lousy attitude, I have a feeling she'll be looking for excuses to get out of the house as often as possible anyway.

24

Neighbor Kid on the Prowl

DEAR ANNIE: I never thought that I would find myself writing to you, but I need advice on how to handle a situation with my neighbors' 10-year-old son.

"Sam" comes into my yard, uninvited, at all hours of the day and night. He has not only climbed my apple trees and loaded his pockets with fruit but also stripped my tomato plants bare, trampled my potato vines and knocked the stuffing out of my scarecrow. On one occasion, I even found him doing his "business" on my begonias! Annie, I was so horrified that I couldn't even speak. When his mother returned home from her yoga class that afternoon, I went over to talk with her. "Boys will be boys!" was about her only response. She also said, "The nanny is supposed to supervise him when he goes out."

I would put up a fence, but my town's zoning ordinances won't allow it. The rest of the neighbors are up in arms about this kid, as well. With gardening season starting again, I am worried that there will be a repeat performance of last year's reign of terror. My garden is my pride and joy, but with Sam on the prowl, not even a scarecrow is safe out there anymore. What can I do?

—*Ready to Throw in the Trowel*

DEAR READY: This little garden gnome has made enough mischief, but his mother is the real troll here. It's time for another chat. Ask what she will do to ensure her son doesn't enter your yard again. This isn't just a matter of manners. If he were to get injured while climbing one of your trees, you could end up facing a lawsuit. Let her know that if he continues to trespass, you will contact local authorities. Good luck to you—and to your scarecrow.

Deciding Where Possessions Will Go

DEAR ANNIE: Please settle a disagreement between my elder sister and me. We will abide by your decision. I recently turned 85 and don't expect to see Christmas, as I am in very poor health. I have been passing heirlooms on to family members, primarily to my granddaughters and their kids, as I lost my eldest son in the early '80s to AIDS and my daughter in 2012 to alcohol.

I want to give my coin collection and gold watches to my ex-son-in-law, my granddaughters' father. Even though he and my daughter divorced 40 years ago, he has always treated me very well, so much better than my daughter did. I've known him since he and my daughter were 15, and he has always been polite and considerate, sending my husband and me photos of our grandkids and great-grandkids over the years. When we couldn't attend his eldest daughter's wedding, he sent us a beautiful video of the event. When we would attend a family function at one of his daughters' homes, he and his current wife would talk to me and listen to my family history stories. If not for my granddaughters and their father, I don't know what I would have done.

I have always admired the relationship he has with his daughters and grandkids and the way he cares for his wife. It is such a great pleasure to be in their presence and see the family life they enjoy.

My sister says that to give my things to my ex-son-in-law would be a slap in the face to my late daughter. My sister has always disapproved of my daughter's marriage, even though

26

she knows what a fine man he is. He already has some collectable coins, and I think he would appreciate mine. So what do you think? Should I give my things to him?

—*Wish I Could Give Him More*

DEAR WICGHM: Your possessions are yours to give. It doesn't matter what anyone else thinks—not your sister and not me, either. But since you asked, I will say that your former son-in-law sounds like a wonderful man, and I think passing these heirlooms down to him would be a sweet way to honor the special friendship you've shared throughout the years. Sweeter still, he actually collects coins, so you can be sure he'll treasure the collection.

No, I'm Not Inbred

DEAR ANNIE: The first meeting of my girlfriend and a couple with whom I am friends caused me to want to retreat into a hole.

My male friend is an intelligent, educated man who is extremely successful in business and recognized as such in the community.

My girlfriend's parents live in West Virginia, of which my male friend became aware. On this, their first meeting, he felt it appropriate to tell West Virginia jokes during dinner, focusing on the offensive stereotypes that residents of the state commonly commit incest and have few or no teeth.

I later apologized to my girlfriend on his behalf. She

graciously said that she is accustomed to such "humor." What does one do in a situation such as this to avoid having the evening collapse?

—Unamused

DEAR UNAMUSED: The joke is on your friend, who fancies himself a cultured man of the world yet showed just how incredibly close-minded he is. Grace doesn't have a ZIP code. True class, intelligence and poise can come from anywhere. Your girlfriend is living proof. It was kind of her to take his remarks in stride.

Your friend should be embarrassed for telling such jokes. They're even more trite than they are insulting. Talk to him about retiring this material.

Guest With a Gross Habit

DEAR ANNIE: My middle-aged confirmed bachelor brother-in-law is a frequent and welcome dinner guest at our house. Lately, when no one is here but his brother and me, he's begun cleaning his plate with his finger and then licking his finger. Sometimes he just licks his plate.

He is a dear. He's also sensitive and easily hurt. I'm reluctant to say anything that might drive him away, and my husband doesn't want to mention it, either. But this unwelcome attention to the last drops of his food makes my stomach churn.

I'm hoping that if you print this, he'll take the hint—and

maybe other food lovers will examine their etiquette, as well.

—*Grossed Out in Georgia*

DEAR GROSSED OUT: This is a classic etiquette conundrum in which calling out the offensive behavior would be ruder than the behavior itself. So I think you'll have to continue to bite your tongue and avert your gaze on this one. And perhaps it will be easier to stomach if you consider what a compliment it is to your cooking.

Invited to Reception But Not Ceremony

DEAR ANNIE: I have a friend who is planning to have her wedding at a lake next year in a state where neither she nor her fiancé lives or has relatives. Her plan is to hold a very small (with about 10 people) private ceremony, to be followed by a reception with about 150 people.

My question is: Is this proper? All the guests are coming from out of state. Shouldn't all the guests be invited to the ceremony? I don't feel it's my place to tell the bride-to-be what I think, but I'm disappointed. I always look forward to the actual wedding ceremony more than the reception. Is that just me?

—*Confused Guest-to-Be*

DEAR CONFUSED: Yes, you're right that typically, everyone would be invited to the ceremony. If anything, I've seen more weddings where the reverse is done—where more people are free to come to the ceremony than the reception because of budget constraints. (How generous of this couple to want to include everyone in the free dinner and drinks part!)

For whatever reason, the bride and groom want to keep the ceremony private. It might not be the traditional choice, but it's their choice.

Don't take this as your being excluded. It's still important to them that you all share in this day. It sounds as if they're looking at the party not merely as a reception but as a celebration of their love in its own right. That's special. Have fun.

Pay Your Way

DEAR ANNIE: I am here wondering: How many times do you go out to eat and expect a free meal? Never, right? So I am really baffled by how someone could attend a wedding (either single or with a date) and find it acceptable to leave a gift of just $100 for two people, let alone $0.

Sure, there are certain financial circumstances that may hinder someone's ability to contribute. But here is my stance: If you can't afford to cover your plate, why go?

A wedding is intended to be a celebration unifying the new couple's lives together. It is not a foundation they set up to make donations for their guests and give them free meals.

It's expensive; everyone knows this. Regardless of who pays for the event, I find it appalling that so many adults would not properly contribute in any fashion—and not even feel embarrassed about it! Maybe their parents fell short in the manners department when raising them.

After being a part of several weddings, I am seriously perplexed by this lack of etiquette. It's very disappointing.

I'm now planning my own wedding, and I find myself left with the dilemma of not wanting to invite certain individuals because I know they wouldn't give any sort of gift. The most upsetting part is this happens to be the case with several of my family members (who are in good positions financially). I know I really can't address it among them, but this has happened at two of my siblings' weddings, and I know it would occur for mine. I don't want to cut family members off, but if they wouldn't contribute, then I feel that I am left without a choice. What do I do?

—Tired of Wedding Freeloaders

DEAR TIRED: Are you planning a wedding or running a business?

It's common courtesy to bring a gift to a wedding, sure. I agree with you 100 percent. But you can't be so concerned with the return on investment. Invite your loved ones because you love them and want them at your wedding, not because you'll get your money's worth. Ultimately, taking the high road will make you feel like a million bucks.

Picked Up a Bug at a Hospital

DEAR ANNIE: I spent some time in the hospital and befriended the woman in the room next to me. We also became friends on Facebook and have kept in touch that way.

I have been having some family problems and decided to move out of my situation, but I couldn't afford to live on my own. A friend from school was also looking to move out of her situation, so we thought that maybe we could share an apartment together. The problem is that when my school friend and I started looking for apartments, my hospital friend suggested we check out an apartment in the building her daughter manages. But the apartment was very disgusting, and we decided not to take it. Well, my hospital friend got very angry and said she didn't want to talk to me anymore. But a few days later, she started chatting with me again.

Now she's back in the hospital, and I have been trying to visit with her, but she's kind of far from my new apartment, and it's been hard. I did visit with her on a Wednesday for three hours. The day after that, I had to go back into the area to pick up a prescription. But I didn't stop in for a visit because I had visited the day before. When she found out that I was in the area and didn't visit, she got angry and asked why. I told her it was because I had just visited the day before. She told me that if it's such a bother to visit, then I should stay away and never visit or talk with her again.

What should I do, apologize and try to visit or do as she said and stay away?

—A Questionable Friend

DEAR QUESTIONABLE: You made it out of the hospital,

but you picked up a bug while you were there. I'm sure this woman is lonely. But that doesn't make it OK for her to try to control you. You've been plenty kind, but it's still not enough for her. She won't be happy until she's sucked up all your time and energy; sounds more like a parasite than a friend. Detox and rid yourself of this unhealthy "friendship."

Roommate Doesn't Want to Split Costs

DEAR ANNIE: My girlfriend and I have another roommate in a two-bedroom place. I usually go to Costco for the household necessities, such as toilet paper and paper towels, because it's cheaper. The three of us split the cost evenly to make the math easy.

This time around, our roommate decided to go to a fancy-schmancy supermarket and pay exorbitant prices for organic versions of the same household items we previously bought at Costco. He even bought two-ply toilet paper that came from a recycled rainforest or something instead of our usual off-brand single-ply.

We had no idea he was going to blow the bank on non-GMO, eco-friendly coffee filters, but when he came home, he gave us the receipt and asked us to split it with him. The total cost was three times what we usually spend.

I feel awkward. He should have told me he was going. I would have suggested Costco. I don't want to split it three ways, because I don't think it's fair. On the other hand, I don't want to just stick him with the bill.

—Frugal Roommate

DEAR FRUGAL: You need to take an economy-sized chill pill. If you feel as if you are acting like a jerk about it, then you probably are acting like a jerk.

Your roommate was just trying to be helpful. Pay your third of the expenses—with no griping. Then discuss setting a budget for household items. Instead of being forced to go to Costco, he's free to shop wherever he wants, as long as he doesn't exceed the budget. Don't be such a control freak. And that fancy two-ply toilet paper may make you more comfortable when you sit down to discuss this, so remember, little luxuries can go a long way.

Man Wants to Say the Right Things

DEAR ANNIE: Recent revelations regarding sexual harassment have prompted me to examine some of my own behavior and actions as they relate to women.

I have never raped or knowingly sexually harassed any woman. I have always held women in high regard and tried to treat them with respect and decency. However, I have said some things and acted in certain ways that may have been questionable, though they have been combined with both humor and sincerity. I would like you and your readers to comment on them.

I have, on many occasions, told women in my workplace that they look attractive, most often citing their outfit. On other occasions, I have done the same with women I don't know. But I have always prefaced my remarks with a qualifying statement, such as "I hope you won't be offended or take this the wrong way," and then added, "But I would like to say how lovely you look."

Also, on other occasions, when I have discerned that they are not offended, I have added in a very clearly humorous voice, "Are you married?" If the answer is "no," I might say, "If you are not busy this weekend, then can we elope!"

If the answer is "yes," I might smilingly and humorously ask, "Well, do you fool around?" Usually, it provokes a laugh and smile.

Now, with the emergence of "Me Too" and all of the awakening consciousness of women—which I wholeheartedly support—I am wondering whether my remarks have been inappropriate or may be interpreted as a form of unwanted sexual advance. I want to do the right thing.

Comments from you and/or your readers would be greatly appreciated. Thank you.

—*A Woman Lover*

DEAR WOMAN LOVER: Yes, these comments probably make the women you work with uncomfortable, and if they laugh, it's probably because they're not sure what else to do. Everyone wants to get along with her co-workers, after all; no one wants to be perceived as harsh or humorless. Try fostering camaraderie in the office without sexual innuendo. Ask about women's families, pets, movie recommendations, upcoming vacations, holiday plans, etc. Though the rules are less strict outside the workplace, err on the side of caution, and don't linger after paying a compliment as if you expect something in return.

One final word to the wise: In any context, if you preface a remark with "Don't take this the wrong way," it will most likely be taken the wrong way.

Tardy to the Party

DEAR ANNIE: I have a friend who is always late. Lunch, dinner, concerts, movies—I don't think I've ever gone to an outing with her when she hasn't shown up 10 or 15 minutes late. She's a lovely, caring person otherwise and a thoughtful friend, but I can't help but be put off by this seeming lack of consideration for other people's time, again and again. It's hard not to take it personally.

She knows it's a problem and has vowed to be more punctual. It was her New Year's resolution last year, and it probably will be again this year, but I'm not holding my breath for change. I just want to know: What gives? Why are some people always late?

—Waiting Games

DEAR WAITING GAMES: According to time management expert Diana DeLonzor, people who are chronically tardy tend to be optimists. They have unrealistic expectations of what they can get done in a set amount of time. Jeff Conte, an associate professor of psychology at San Diego State, says lateness is connected to deep-seated personality factors, making it a very hard habit to break. So your friend's chronic tardiness is likely as deeply embedded in her as the things you love about her. Keeping all that in mind might make it easier not to take it personally when she's late—but she can't expect everyone to be so understanding. DeLonzor's book, "Never Be Late Again," might make a good holiday gift for your friend, seeing as she admits it's a problem.

Ruffling Some Feathers

DEAR ANNIE: I was at my brother's home for my sister-in-law's birthday a few weeks ago. My sister-in-law, "Jess," had a stroke some years ago and can only say a few single-syllable words at a time. She has an 18-year-old bird that she loves and takes care of.

My nephew's fiancé, "Becky," and her daughter, "Emily," came over during the party, and Emily started to tease the bird. Jess looked at me and said, "Cover bird." I went over and very politely put the cover on the birdcage and said, "I think it's time for the bird to go to sleep. When there are a lot of people in the house, the bird gets stressed out. The cover helps him calm down."

Everything was fine for about 10 minutes. But then Emily went over, flipped part of the cover off the cage and started to tease the bird again. Becky was sitting right there and did not say a word to her daughter. I looked on silently because I felt it was not my place to say anything, and Emily sat down after a few minutes anyway.

But then she went over to the cage a third time. She began teasing the bird. At this point, my brother politely told Emily to stop because she was upsetting the bird, and she did.

37

At that point, Becky got upset. She told my brother, "She's only playing with the bird." She and Emily left the birthday party early because of this.

My brother and I would like you opinion on whether or not it was inappropriate for him to tell Emily to stop.

—*Birdy-guard*

DEAR BIRDY-GUARD: Of course it was appropriate of your brother to speak up. If that ruffled Becky's feathers, she should have stepped in before he had to. The next time you're all together, set some ground rules right from the start, and make them clear to Emily, Becky and your nephew: no ifs, ands or squawks about it.

That's My Spot!

DEAR ANNIE: When it's snowed and you've shoveled clear a parking place for yourself, is it OK for other people to park in the spot you've cleared when you're elsewhere and not occupying it? What is the common courtesy that should be adhered to?

Recently, our town had over 16 inches of snow. My friend is a single mom in her mid-40s who is undergoing chemotherapy for breast cancer. She rents her home and has no off-street parking. Her teenage son shoveled a parking space for her in front of their residence along the public street. She left in her vehicle for one of her treatments, and upon returning, she found that a vehicle was parked in the spot her son had shoveled out, and there were no more shoveled-out spaces.

She was extremely upset by this unkind gesture and posted her feelings on Facebook, where she received many responses from people who were angry on her behalf. Their suggestions included covertly doing destructive things to the car that had parked in her spot. Someone suggested covering the vehicle back up with snow. Other people suggested placing cinder blocks or traffic cones within the space to keep others from using it.

I have mixed feelings on this. Although in a perfect world common courtesy would always be observed, reality says that it is, after all, public parking along a public street, and the person who parked there had no idea of my friend's personal situation. That driver simply saw a nice open place to park.

During this snowstorm, I am sure there were many people angry and frustrated with similar situations, especially people who are elderly or handicapped. I completely sympathize with the frustration, but I'm not sure what could have been done.

—Thinking Person in Pennsylvania

DEAR THINKING: I'm with you. The person who took your friend's spot most likely thought nothing other than, "Lucky me!" We humans tend to be self-absorbed that way, unfortunately.

Shoveling snow back onto the car would have been vindictive and would have required a lot of effort just for the sake of being petty. Putting cones or cinder blocks as place holders would have sent a clearer message that it was reserved, but it wouldn't have stopped any truly inconsiderate person from parking there anyway.

In many cities throughout the U.S., a person with a disability can apply to have a handicapped parking space designated on the street outside his or her home if off-street parking isn't available. There are restrictions on eligibility. (Some cities disqualify people who will have a DMV-issued disability placard for less than a year.) Check your city's website for more information.

Overeager Listener

DEAR ANNIE: Do you know of any etiquette guidelines for speaking with someone who has a stutter or another speech impediment? I recently befriended a man from the neighborhood who has a stutter. I have a bad habit of finishing other people's sentences in general, and I find myself wanting to jump in and help him complete his thought when he pauses. I'm assuming that is considered rude.

—Wondering

DEAR WONDERING: The etiquette for talking to someone who stutters is the same as the etiquette for talking to someone who doesn't. Listen; be patient; make eye contact; and ask for clarification if you missed something. Don't interrupt, finish his sentences or rush him to get to the point. The only difference is that it's more important to observe that decorum when talking to someone who stutters, lest you come off as patronizing.

I believe that your friend came into your life for a reason—to

40

teach you patience and the lost art of holding one's tongue. Be a good listener to him and you'll become a better communicator with anyone.

Revisiting 'Thank You' Etiquette

DEAR ANNIE: Seven months after attending a wedding, I just received a computer-generated thank-you note. The note was printed on a label and then stuck on a purchased note card.

Although it addressed us by name, it never acknowledged any gift given. It simply said they appreciated our "sharing (our) generosity" and thanked us for being part of their day and for being in their lives. Also included was a tiny picture of the couple. There were fewer than 100 guests at the wedding, so the couple were not overwhelmed with thank-you notes to write. The groom's parents are great friends of ours, and we gave the gift to them prior to the wedding, but we're now left wondering: Did the couple actually get the gift and know it was from us? Do I say something to the groom's parents, and if so, how do I tactfully say this?

I would hate to think that this is the new trend among young brides. Thankfully, I know three recent young brides who were very prompt with their notes and personalized their messages.

—Confused in Connecticut

DEAR CONFUSED: They probably received your gift; they

just never got their manners. There's no real tactful way to speak to the groom's parents about this issue, so I would just let it go. As a poet wrote nearly 1,000 years ago, "the test of good manners is to be patient with the bad ones."

Brand-new newlyweds: Please handwrite your thank-you notes. It's easier to deal with a cramped hand for a day than guests feeling slighted for years.

Troublesome Co-Worker

DEAR ANNIE: I'm having issues with my co-worker. I am maybe three or four years older than she is. This is her first job, but she has been here for two or three years. I have had many jobs previously, and I have been here for about a year now. She is a woman who has that "anything you can do I can do better" attitude toward men and does the hardest jobs to prove herself.

For the past several months, she has been actively avoiding me. It started when she would come up to others near me and invite them to parties and just ignore that I was there— consistently excluding me from these talks. It's not that bad to be excluded; we don't have to be friends. But it's more than that now. I can't remember the last time she spoke to me, even when communication between us has been crucial for us to do our jobs. If I go to the break room, the smoking area or the bathroom at the same time she does, she will straight up book it out of there, not looking at me, not speaking to me. I have no idea why!

She calls our supervisor to complain about me. Now I am careful about what I say and how I say it. I am always nice to her and friendly. She has called managers, in front of me, to ask them to tell me to do a task that I clearly was about to do already. I've told her a few times that she could just radio me instead of going through the extra step of having the supervisor tell me. She says she will talk to me directly next time.

An hour later, I get a call to the office, and the managers say she came in to complain about my "confronting" her. It's in no way a confrontation. I wish they would call us both up so we could talk it out in the office.

I don't know why she is doing stuff like this to me. Every time I try to talk to her, she gives me a curt answer and takes off. Nothing gets done, and this trying to get me in trouble thing she's on now is ridiculous. One of my supervisors gets it, and I know he knows this is happening. The other, I think, may be more on her side. I am going to leave this job soon for other reasons, but any advice on what I can do here?

—What Did I Do?

DEAR WDID: This woman can point her finger only so many times before the higher-ups notice that the rest of her fingers are pointed back at herself. You might speak to the human resources department and ask for some mediation and guidance. But if you're leaving soon anyway, keep your head down and work hard. Ignore her antics. And give a professional but frank assessment of her in your exit interview.

To Go to Wedding or Not

DEAR ANNIE: My stepson was married in a small backyard ceremony. His father and I were not invited and were not even aware of the wedding until after it was over. Now, a year and a half later, we are invited to a "wedding reception." He lives in another state, and it is very difficult to travel (for health and money reasons). I don't want to go, but my husband insists we go. I won't know many people, but all his ex-wife's family will be there, and they are not very nice.

What can I do? The parties will be in a place I cannot stand to be. Should I grit my teeth and suffer through the long car ride and the rest? If he goes without me, his ex will be all over him. (It's happened before, right in front of me.) What to do?

—*Wary and Weary Traveler*

DEAR WARY: You may want to pick up a mouthguard, because yes, I think you have to grit your teeth through this one. When you marry someone, you also marry his family. If it's possible to overcome the health and financial issues (and it sounds as if it is, seeing as your husband is set on going), then go. It's just one weekend. Your husband should appreciate the effort on your part for a long time.

Trumpeter in Turmoil

DEAR ANNIE: I've been a successful trumpet player for five years now and in marching band for three. My director praises me often and says I've shown much improvement since last year.

However, despite my being great and all, there is a problem: a 5-foot-tall trumpet-playing problem. "Addie" has been in concert band for a year and in marching band for about two years. She has been up the director's rear end ever since our winter concert last December about being a trumpet in the halftime show.

Recently, as the director and I were discussing halftime show music, Addie came up and inserted herself into the conversation. Then she and the director talked, and it was decided that I would be on second trumpet.

I have been working hard to be first trumpet in the halftime show for years now, and I wasn't going to let Addie steal that from me. After my mom had a discussion with our director (even though I told her not to), we all agreed on splitting up the parts. I mainly have the second trumpet part, except for three songs in both pregame and halftime. I was given the solo I had wanted so badly, and I'm also part of a brass quintet in another halftime song. (Addie got an eight-measure feature in that song, which she brags about daily.)

But still, I feel that she's trying to steal my part. She played my solo the other day while the high brass members were just messing around and said, "Ha! That's fun. I can see why you like to play it." I'm unsure whether she's trying to one-up me or trying to support me. What should I say to her to get her to stop?

—*Band Geek in a Bad Mood*

DEAR BAND GEEK: That football field is big enough for the both of you. I doubt Addie is out to get you, but even if she were, you can't stop a one-upper by one-upping her. Instead, focus on practicing even harder. If you channel your competitive energy into becoming your best rather than besting somebody else, it will pay off.

Requests for Rutabagas

DEAR ANNIE: Every year, I grow a beautiful vegetable garden. It's a hobby, as well as therapy, and I enjoy it very much. I generously share my fresh produce with family, friends and many neighbors. However, I have a couple of neighbors who ask repeatedly for veggies. (Something I would never have the nerve to do!)

These "requests" always catch me off guard, so I give in.

I feel that it should be my idea when, what, how much and with whom I share my garden bounty. Am I wrong? What can I tell these folks when they come begging?

—*Mrs. Greenthumb*

DEAR MRS. GREENTHUMB: It seems that these pesky neighbors took your past offers of vegetables as an open invitation. Make a point of closing it. The next time they ask, say that you have no veggies to spare now but that you'll be sure to let them know if you do in the future.

Wedding Gifts

DEAR ANNIE: I was recently married and had a big, fancy, expensive wedding. I limited guests to close friends, relatives and just a few "friends" from work. The cost per plate was $125.

Here is the problem: One of the "friends" from work I invited was with her on-again, off-again boyfriend at the time. After receiving her invitation, she asked me at work whether she could bring him. I was a little put back, as it was an expensive wedding and I had not originally included her boyfriend because they were not in a committed relationship. Being put on the spot, I told her she could bring him.

Well, the wedding came, and they both came, ate, drank at the free open bar and danced.

After our honeymoon, my husband and I opened all the cards and gifts. There was nothing from her, not even a card. I double-checked and triple-checked just to make sure I was not missing a card from her.

It's not that I was expecting a present, but I thought it rude and unusual for a guest to not even bring a card. I never said anything to her about it but rather stayed cool toward her afterward. The question is: Should I have said something to her about it? Is this the new norm, to come to an expensive wedding and not even bring a card?

—*Wondering in Upstate New York*

DEAR WONDERING: Traditional etiquette holds that guests have up to one year after a wedding to send a gift, although ideally they should send their gifts within two months. It's very possible that your gift will arrive any day now, so warm back up to your co-worker.

She Makes How Much?

DEAR ANNIE: I have 38 years of experience in the health care industry. I love my job and co-workers. I've been at my present job for 11 years. "Good work ethics, dependability, loyalty and honesty" is my work mantra. My co-worker "Samantha" has been here for a little over two years. She is doing a great job. Our duties are comparable. I enjoy working with her and care for her very much.

But she is a very close friend of my employer's and of my office manager's, and some time ago, I learned that she is making the same hourly wage as I am. Her past experience was teaching preschool.

Needless to say, it has been hurtful; I feel slighted, and it has rattled my work confidence. Over the past 10 years, I have turned down three job offers that would have paid me a higher wage. My employer doesn't know this or realize my loyalty to the office. Retirement is three or four years away for me, but in the meantime, I would like to be treated fairly, and I don't know how to handle this situation. Could you please offer me a solution or some advice?

—Undervalued

DEAR UNDERVALUED: Your experience speaks to the power of perspective. You went from being extremely satisfied to feeling cheated, not because of any change in your job or the way your employer treated you but because you gained knowledge about your co-worker's salary. Still, I understand why you're irritated.

If you haven't gotten a raise in a while, now is the perfect time to request one. Highlight your dedication and work ethic to your manager just as you did in your letter. And if you don't get the answer you're looking for, make peace with the situation. Get back to your mantra. Keep your eyes on the horizon and that promising rainbow that is retirement. You're fortunate to have a job you love enough to turn down higher-paying offers. Not many people can say that.

Night at the Mall

DEAR ANNIE: My 13-year-old daughter has been invited to her classmate's birthday party. The mom of the birthday girl plans to drop off the girls at the mall—six of them—for four hours, during which they'll wander around with money, cellphones, credit cards and a plan to get food at some point.

I am not comfortable with this. I called the mom and asked why she isn't going with them. Her daughter doesn't want her there. I suggested the two of us go with the girls and perhaps even let them go off on their own for short periods and meet up with them a few times. But no. She wants her daughter to feel "independent" and to give her her "space."

Besides the safety issue, I don't like the idea of just going to the mall to hang out. Not much good comes from that. My daughter always comes home wanting a bunch of stuff she doesn't need. When she buys clothes or junk impulsively, it always ends up in the trash or on the charity pile a few months later. We're on a tight budget, and this is not in it. I don't mind getting her friend a birthday gift, but that's different.

If it were anyone else, we'd just skip it. But this is her closest friend, so it would be devastating for both of them if she didn't go. But I really don't want her to go under these circumstances.

—*Between a Rock and a Hard Place in Ohio*

DEAR BETWEEN: Personally, I think your suggestion to the mom was a bright idea. That being said, it's her daughter's birthday, and they can do what they want. Likewise, you can make choices about what's right for your own family. If this mall idea is absolutely unacceptable to you, you are entitled to put your foot down and explain that different families have different rules.

But if you'd like to make an exception and let your daughter attend, lay down some ground rules to help her be safe and responsible. 1) She can only spend her own money—and not too much of it. Set a limit you feel is fair, such as $30-50. 2) Cash only. No credit cards. 3) Have her call to check in with you halfway through the night, perhaps while they're eating dinner. There will come a time when she's be out shopping without her mom, so this could be the perfect opportunity to practice good habits.

When HR Is the Problem

DEAR ANNIE: We work in a small office with just over 20

employees. It has recently become common knowledge that the human resources manager, "Melissa," is sleeping with the principal in our firm, "Larry."

Throughout her eight years with this private firm, the closed-door huddles were always viewed as suspect, but they were both married, and those of us naive enough to assume the best hoped that it was professional. The timeline is fuzzy, but Melissa's divorce seemed to follow the beginning of the now-three-year affair by about a year. Larry's divorce is not yet final.

Regardless, Melissa has never been seen as an effective HR representative. There are several reasons for that, but it's mainly because of her obvious familiarity with Larry. With the revelation of their affair, she's lost all remaining credibility in her role. Is there a standard of ethics for an HR department?

It's a department of one, so where should we employees turn with an issue that clearly could not be handled by her with an unbiased, disentangled perspective? Their dirty laundry is having an unnerving effect on everyone.

—Unrepresented

DEAR UNREPRESENTED: Shame on these two for letting their dirty laundry stink up the whole office. They should know better. Melissa's job as the HR representative is to regulate fraternization, not engage in it. If there is anyone above or equal to Larry's ranking, anonymously report your concerns. If Larry doesn't recognize the error of his ways yet, he'll soon see the consequences unfold throughout the company. Such unsavory behavior is toxic to morale.

Get Off Your Property!

DEAR ANNIE: We have some new neighbors, and our backyards are adjoining. We enjoy sitting out on our deck on nice evenings and enjoying the weather with a drink and snack. Sometimes friends stop by. We are quiet and aren't out late. Our neighbors have several young children, and they are outdoors all the time. We're not thrilled with the constant noise, but we put up with it. We've tried to remain friendly and polite. Recently, there's a new issue: Our neighbors informed us that it's "creepy and inappropriate" when we sit outside when the kids are out playing and that we shouldn't be doing so because it makes them uncomfortable. We're sitting in our lounge chairs and not even facing their direction. We can't put up a taller privacy fence or plant bushes because of a city ordinance, so if we can't use our deck when the kids are outdoors, we won't be able to use it at all.

We're not sure what to do. We feel that we're being bullied and that we're doing nothing wrong, but if the family were to become angry and accuse us of something, our lives would be ruined. We love this house but feel that our only option at this point is to move. However, that would leave the next owners in the same predicament. I took some muffins over and tried to explain to the mother that we mean no harm to the children—that we're just enjoying our deck on our property—and she asked me to leave, saying, "The kids will be home from school soon."

I did visit our local police department to talk about the accusation, and an officer said we'd better just stay inside to prevent escalation. But who's to say these neighbors won't decide (falsely) that we're watching their kids through the windows? This whole situation makes us very uncomfortable, and we're not sure what to do.

—Housebound Through No Fault of Our Own in Iowa

DEAR HOUSEBOUND: Relaxing on the deck at dusk after a good dinner—that's one of life's simple pleasures. Don't let the oddballs next door deprive you of that. You've done nothing wrong. If you want some privacy for your own peace of mind, try lining the side of your deck that faces them with large potted plants, or consider installing a canopy from which you could drape some curtains. If they continue to harangue you, tell them you'll stop sitting in your backyard when they show you the penal code that says you can't.

You're Eating That?

DEAR ANNIE: I work in an office with mostly wonderful ladies with whom I, in general, get along well with. I have one lunchtime irritation.

There is a certain co-worker, "June," who always has a comment to make about what I'm eating for lunch. She never says anything so blunt as, "That is unhealthy! How can you eat that?!" However, her comments often make me feel that she actually thinks that. She will make a remark such as, "Oh, pasta? Well, I guess that tastes better than my protein smoothie."

I know that in itself, that is a pretty innocent comment and nothing to get flustered over, but it happens every time she and I have the same lunch hour—or even when she happens to walk in the break room while I'm on lunch. Several times, she has even made a joke when I've ordered from the sandwich shop across the street (which I do only once or twice a month), saying that I must be single-handedly keeping the place in business.

I realize that I may be being overly sensitive, but I just feel that people should have more tact when talking about what others eat. Actually, I don't see the need for others to ever comment about that at all! Why do people think that is OK? And do you have a suggestion for how I could tactfully tell June that her comments really bother me?

—*Fed Up*

DEAR FED: June needs to mind her own lunchbox. It sounds as if she is fixated with dieting and is envious of your ability to enjoy what you eat. I don't think she's consciously trying to make you feel bad, so you might first try gently bringing her attention to what she's doing.

Every time she mentions how good your lunch looks, offer her some. She'll most likely decline and for a moment be forced to consider why she made the comment in the first place.

If the comments persist, then it's time to be direct. Let her know that you're sensitive to the remarks about your diet and that you'd appreciate her not commenting on your lunch unless she's asking for the recipe.

The Other Side of the Law

DEAR ANNIE: I bet you're surprised right now, and I don't blame you. I know it is not an everyday type of thing to receive mail from an inmate. I read your section of the newspaper every week and have to admit that it's pretty interesting.

I'm a 19-year-old man currently residing in this lovely facility, facing four years and eight months for robbery and possession of a controlled substance for sale, with a gang enhancement and a bail enhancement. I stress about my case often. That has nothing to do with the amount of time I'm serving, because I can do that standing up; all I've got to do is count my blessings and tell myself that there are people in here who aren't ever going home. But sadly, there's a possibility of my joining them because I've taken two strikes at such a young age.

I know I have to change my ways, and I wouldn't have to worry about anything if I did, but I'll be honest: I won't change. I chose this lifestyle, and it's all I know. I don't want to change, either. I just want to know one thing: Do you think I'm wrong?

I'm so confused. I think you should put this in the newspaper and show people some real stress and some real advice. I see you throwing light into dark situations with the flick of your tongue and would appreciate some help.

—*Confused Young Life in California*

DEAR CONFUSED: You are so young, and I promise you that the world is so much bigger than it seems right now. You can still be whoever you want. And I think that deep down, a part of you does want to change, or you wouldn't be writing me.

The most important factors will be the people you surround yourself with and the help you seek in your first year out of prison, especially during the first few weeks and months. There are a number of resources for people in your shoes in California, such as the Men of Valor Academy (510-567-1308) and the Center for Employment Opportunities (510-251-2240). Please don't give up on yourself.

Readers: If you have been in a similar position and turned things around, I would love to hear from you.

Limiting Identity Theft

DEAR ANNIE: I would like to remind readers not to carry their Social Security cards in their wallets, because if a card is lost or stolen, a person could become the victim of identity theft. On numerous occasions, I have had transactions with an elderly gentleman, and each time he opens his wallet, I see his Social Security card prominently displayed under a window sleeve.

On one visit, I very nicely mentioned how the card should be locked in a safe in his home and why. He said he sometimes needs to give out his Social Security number. I told him it should be memorized and it's never necessary to actually show the card. I've waited on him several times since, and I still see his card on each visit.

Please, readers, make sure your loved ones do not carry their cards on them and they are locked away in a safe place.

Unfortunately, identity theft is very prevalent, and crooks will stop at nothing to find their next victim.

—Waits on Customers in VA

DEAR WAITS ON CUSTOMERS: I second your plea. According to the Identity Theft Resource Center, "identity theft springing from a stolen Social Security card carried in a wallet or purse is among the most common ways people become victims." If you've lost your Social Security card—even if you don't believe it's being used—call the Social Security Administration at 800-772-1213. If your card has been stolen, contact your local police department immediately, and visit https://identitytheft.gov for more steps you can take after the fact.

Putting on Shoes and Socks

DEAR ANNIE: Is there a right order and a wrong order for putting on one's shoes and socks? I find that on most days, I put on both socks and then both shoes. The other day, I put on one sock and one shoe and then the other sock and other shoe. I remember a scene on the old TV show "All in the Family" in which Archie Bunker and Meathead were getting ready to go out. Archie noticed that Meathead had put on one sock and one shoe, and Archie asked him what he was doing. Why didn't he put on both socks first and then the shoes? "I like to take care of one foot at a time," Meathead says. It was really funny. (The clip is available on YouTube, titled "Archie Bunker—A Sock And A Sock And A Shoe And A Shoe!")

But I am wondering whether any polling company has ever done a survey of how people put on their shoes and socks.

—Curious in Klamath Falls

DEAR CURIOUS: Don't know of any survey, but I suspect that most people dress in the order Archie does. In my view, as long as each shoe ends up on its correct foot, you're doing all right. However, if any of my readers feel strongly about the one-sock-one-shoe method, I'd love to hear from you.

◆

DO WE OWE OUR CHILDREN MONEY TO LAUNCH THEIR CAREERS?

Family

Biological Schmiological

DEAR ANNIE: My husband and I have been together for eight years, and we have one child together. I also have a 9-year-old from a previous relationship. My husband is the only father my 9-year-old has ever known. He calls him Daddy.

The problem is my mother-in-law. She has stated that she has "no ties" to my son. She will not invite him over or do things with him the way she does with my younger child (her biological grandson). She doesn't ask questions about him as she does with my younger child, and recently she didn't even bother to call and tell him happy birthday. She posted "Happy Birthday" on Facebook, but that was it. Her current husband also has a grandson, and she will have him come stay with them anytime.

My son doesn't seem to be too bothered by the way she treats him. (He has autism but is higher-functioning.) But a few months ago, my younger son spent some time with my mother-in-law, and a few days later, I overheard him talking to my elder son. He said, "You should have gone shopping with me and Mimi, but she doesn't want you there." That broke my heart.

I've let my younger son have a relationship with her. I do it more for him than for her. I don't want him to be resentful that he never got to spend time with his grandmother, but at the same time, I feel that it's hurting my other child, even though he doesn't verbally express it.

I know that my mother-in-law is not supportive of her son's being married to me. She has never liked me from day one. She even had the nerve to once tell my own mother that I am nothing but trailer trash. Of course, that's far from the truth. I did have a child when I was 18, but I've worked hard and I've been a great mom. I graduated high school, and I started college when my son was only 20 days old and worked full time, as well. I met my husband when I was 19, and we have been together ever since. I am currently working full time and going to school part time.

I have come to believe I will never be good enough in her eyes. I'm working on accepting that, but it's hard. My husband says he has talked to her several times, but there has been no change in her behavior. I've told her how I feel, and she said that she is always going to show favoritism. What do I do from here? Let it go? Stay away? Kill her with kindness?

—*Trying Not to Be Bitter*

DEAR TRYING: Have you ever seen your mother-in-law in rain? Because she sounds like the Wicked Witch. Exclusion of any kind or purposeful cruelty is never OK, in my book.

Good for you for not resigning yourself to anger and bitterness. That takes a lot of strength. It sounds as if you've tried to be patient and made a real effort to have a better relationship with your mother-in-law. She is, after all, your husband's mom. Unfortunately, she's made no effort to have a better relationship with you. Clearly, your husband's talks with her have had no effect. Actions speak louder than words, and it may be time to pump up the volume.

Grandma shouldn't be allowed to see your younger son until she starts treating your 9-year-old with love and respect. She can't have this sort of a la carte relationship with your family—showing affection to your husband and her biological grandson and none to you and your elder son. You're a package deal. If she can't handle that, she can get onto her broomstick and out of your lives.

A Situation That's Not a Comedy

DEAR ANNIE: For the past two decades, my life has been an episode of the sitcom "Everybody Loves Raymond" on steroids.

My mother-in-law has made a wonderful grandmother, but she has constantly criticized my weight, my hairstyle, what I feed my children and how I dress and discipline them. She always does this out of earshot of her husband and son. I have kept my mouth shut to keep the peace, and I respect my dear father-in-law and husband too much to tell her off and cause a family rift.

Six months ago, she got a Facebook account for the first time. She wrote something rude about another family member, not knowing everyone could see it. We went over to show her how to remove it and explained that the whole world could see her inappropriate comment. She got defensive and called me hurtful names. I called her a troublemaker and walked out.

She hasn't spoken to me since, and neither has my father-in-law. He was not even there, so I can't imagine what she told him. My husband was there and knows I didn't do or say anything wrong and is not reaching out to them because he knows his mother was wrong.

I tried writing my father-in-law a letter but got no response. His alienation hurts me more than anything because I can't believe he would go along with this. I know she will never apologize, but how do we rectify this if they continue to ignore phone calls, cards and letters? They are elderly, and I am afraid something will happen and my husband will live the rest of his life with regret over this

—Daughter-in-Law in the Middle

DEAR DIL: The thing about sitcoms is that no matter how bad a family feud is, everything is neatly restored by the end of the 30-minute time slot, and the studio audience issues a collective "aww." If only.

Your husband has the biggest role here. Encourage him to set his (justified) anger aside and pay his parents a visit. No matter how big a drama queen she is, it will be hard for his mother to slam the door in the face of her baby boy. Once he's made amends, he can help smooth things over for you, too.

I'd also like to say that your husband and in-laws are lucky to have you. You are a tolerant and caring person. Major props for holding the family together.

Daddy's 'Little Girl'

DEAR ANNIE: I am absolutely at my wits' end and seriously thinking of divorcing my husband. My husband and I have been married for 11 years. My stepdaughter is 26. She married three years ago after living with her boyfriend for a year. The problem is that she still places her dad over her husband. Her poor husband takes it because he is very meek and does whatever she wants. She definitely wears the pants in the family. She wants to be married, but she still wants to be Daddy's little girl. It goes beyond that. She still has him so high on a pedestal that it is ridiculous for a supposedly grown woman.

She is driving a definite wedge between us, and it is serious. They live about two hours away. She and her husband both have jobs. Yet she calls and cries tears that she misses her dad. They still have date nights; he has offered to go places with her if she does not want to go alone. If she calls and has a problem or something that needs to be fixed, he drops everything and runs to her. In my opinion, she chose to get married and have a husband. She needs to rely on him for things and cut the apron strings with Daddy some and be an adult. I am not begrudging visits; in fact, I encourage them. But I refuse to change our plans simply because she decides, spur of the moment, to make an appearance. He always takes her side that we should let her come and change our plans. This makes me the monster if I dare say no. I think plans should be made accordingly. We should all four do things together. We could do a dinner out, a day out, etc. My pleas fall on deaf ears.

How do you deal with a 26-year-old who thinks the world revolves around her? I don't see where she and her husband make any attempt to create their own friendships and have their own life. These are supposed to be the happy years when we can go out and do as we please, but it is far from that. I am about to give up and start taking vacations by myself

—*Desperate in Montana*

DEAR DESPERATE: You can take a vacation, but these problems will be waiting for you when you get back. So before you get out the suitcase, try getting in your husband's head. He seems to have a guilt complex that makes him feel the need to bend over backward to make his daughter happy. His fuzzy-headedness on the subject means that you end up having to be the voice of reason—a voice unwelcome to his daughter and therefore unwelcome to him. (He has the overwhelming need to keep her happy, remember.) If you keep fighting the battle this way, you're destined to lose.

Instead, you need to get him on your side of the issue, whether by going to therapy together or just by putting on your own therapist cap and talking it out. Why does he feel compelled to help his daughter all the time? How does he think this will impact her and her marriage in the long run? With some clarity, he should see that this codependent behavior is unhealthy and does his daughter a disservice. She needs to learn how to rely not on her dad or even on her husband but on herself.

Generational Divide About Dating

DEAR ANNIE: I'm lucky in that I feel as if I can talk to my parents about everything—everything, that is, except my dating life. My parents met in high school and got married while still attending their local state college. I'm in my mid-20s, and though I'd like a family one day, I'm currently working on getting my master's degree and working part time. This leaves little room for dating.

My parents get their hopes up every time I tell them I've met a guy, and it crushes me to disappoint them when it doesn't go anywhere. It's tiring trying to explain to my mom that going on a few dates with a guy doesn't mean that we're on the road to marriage. Twenty-first-century dating is so complicated. I can't imagine having a conversation with my mom about navigating Tinder or reading into Instagram likes or being ghosted.

I've stopped telling them about my dating life because it seems easier that way, but it also feels as if I'm hiding part of my life from my parents. Annie, how do I bridge this generational gap?

—Single Sally

DEAR SINGLE: Give your parents more credit, Sally. You think your generation is the first to experience guys disappearing after a few dates? Imagine only having a landline to communicate. Though you don't have to share the nitty-gritty details with your folks, it sounds as if they want to be there for you to share in the good times and the bad. This "gap" is of your own making. Though potentially awkward, explaining dating apps to your mom could be enlightening and even fun.

Your parents should appreciate your dedication to finding the right man, as opposed to just settling down. Better to be the tortoise who takes her time getting married than the hare who's speeding toward her second divorce.

The Real Dad

DEAR ANNIE: When she was 21, our daughter became pregnant by a casual college boyfriend. Three months into her pregnancy, they broke up because the young man had no interest in raising a child. Our daughter decided to let him go and has not ever found him or required child support from him.

During the pregnancy, she began dating another young man, who wasn't put off by the fact that she was pregnant with someone else's baby. He loved our daughter and was committed to raising the baby as his own.

They married soon after our granddaughter was born, and despite divorcing our daughter three years later, our former son-in-law has continued his commitment to being a loving father to our granddaughter. He has been the only father in her life. His parents and family have always loved and included our granddaughter as their own.

Our granddaughter is now 16. No one has ever told her the truth—that our former son-in-law is not her biological father.

Our daughter has done a great job raising her daughter but is terrified of the prospect of telling her daughter the truth. She is afraid her daughter will flip out and hate her when she is told the truth. She also fears her daughter will be angry with everyone who knows the truth and has been "lying" to her all these years.

Our family—and our daughter's ex-husband's family—all agree that our daughter needs to tell her the truth soon,

67

before someone spills the beans and our granddaughter is devastated. But our daughter is passive. She wishes someone else would take care of this for her, but we all agree she needs to be the one to tactfully tell her daughter the truth.

Do you have any advice on how this situation should be handled?

—*Concerned Grandma*

DEAR CONCERNED: Even the best-intentioned secrets are still secrets, and they're dangerous. It's in your granddaughter's best interest to know who her biological father is. However she processes it, it's information she deserves to have, one of the more practical reasons being for the sake of her medical records.

Help your daughter talk through her fears. She's said she is afraid her daughter will flip out, so explore the worst-case scenarios there. She's only 16; she can't very well pack up and start a new life over this news. She might threaten as much, but once the dust settles, she'll still be there, and so will all of you.

As a family, you can reassure her that biology does not make a father. Love and commitment do. The man who tucked her in and read "Green Eggs and Ham," taught her how to ride a bike, kissed her bruises when she fell, spent hours trying to grasp the concepts of geometry so he could help her study, dried her tears when the other kids left her out, dried his own tears on all her first days of school—he is her real father. And that will always be the whole truth.

Pressured to Have Another

DEAR ANNIE: My son just turned 6 months old, and he is my entire world. I love him to pieces, and I love being a mom more than I thought was possible. I also work full time as a science teacher and softball coach at the local middle school. When I get home, I am beyond tired.

My husband and I live very close to where we grew up—we are from the same town but didn't meet till after college—and our families are close by. This is super helpful when it comes to last-minute baby-sitting needs, hand-me-down toys and just being around supportive people. But being this close to our families is creating an issue.

Lately, my mother-in-law won't stop asking me when I'm going to get pregnant again. When I say that we're in no rush, she asks pointed questions. For example, "Don't you love being a mom?" "Don't you want your son to grow up with siblings?" Of course I do! And I do want more children, but, Annie, I'm so drained all the time. And I didn't know the strain that a baby would put on my relationship with my husband. I'm barely holding on as is, and I want to take the time to enjoy being with my son. How do I get my mother-in-law to back off without offending her? I don't want to have another fight. But I'm not ready for another kid, either.

—Tired in Tulsa

DEAR TIRED: Your mother-in-law's pointed questions are best met with a soft—but clear—response. You might say something like, "I am overjoyed by how excited you are to be a grandma. Thank you so much for the help you've given your son and me. We definitely want siblings, but I'm not nearly ready to think about that yet. When I am ready, I promise you'll be the first to know."

If she continues scanning the sky for storks and giving you the third degree, enlist your husband for support. He can get away with being more blunt. After all, he is her baby boy.

The Sleeping Tyrant

DEAR ANNIE: When he is awake, my husband is a mild-mannered person who rarely raises his voice. He is not very talkative and reads most of the day. However, when he sleeps, he becomes someone else. He talks; he laughs; he sings; he argues; he flings his arms around as if trying to fight and talks in a slurred voice as if he were inebriated.

Last night, he sat up in bed and talked a blue streak to the dog, who ran off scared. He has pushed, poked and prodded me in his sleep, which of course awakens me. I am then unable to get back to sleep for hours and am miserable the next day. I fear that his behavior will escalate and become violent. During his episodes, I give him a push, and he usually rolls over and goes back to sleep.

Before bed, he usually drinks one beer, and to help him sleep, he takes one 3-milligram tablet of melatonin. This behavior has evolved over the past year. He is retired and over 80 years old. We have only one bedroom, making it impossible for him to sleep elsewhere. Could this be a medical problem? Should he speak to his general practitioner? Or does he have a split personality that only emerges at night? Any suggestion would be most welcome

—*Tired of Living With Dr. Jekyll and Mr. Hyde*

DEAR TIRED: There are a few possible explanations here, but rest assured that none of them involves your husband's having a split personality. It could be the melatonin. Some people report having extremely vivid and bizarre dreams after taking the sleep aid. If this is the case for your husband, intense dreams could be causing him to act things out physically in his sleep. It's also possible that he suffers from REM sleep behavior disorder or night terrors.

Whatever the cause, the fact that he screams and flails is reason enough to discuss the issue with his doctor, who can refer him to a sleep specialist. If he's resistant to getting help, remind him that this impacts your health, too (lack of sleep can cause a host of health problems)—and he's scaring the poor dog.

In-Laws Ruin the Holidays

DEAR ANNIE: I've been married for almost 20 years, and for all of those years, my in-laws have ruined my holiday season. From the very beginning, I've tried really hard to be gracious, kind and generous. These are all of the attributes that my mother (now deceased) always told me that family is about. I come from a big close-knit family. We all share and contribute not only to family events but also to help one another out in general.

Not my in-laws. My husband and I have hosted or paid for every single meal we've had with them. In fact, they don't call us unless they need something.

My husband has been very protective of my feelings. He is so disgusted by the way they treat all of us that he would like to just cut them off. I can't do it. I keep hearing my mom telling me that this is his family. I think he would regret it later, and I don't want to be the cause.

Let me tell you what a holiday meal is like. I cook all of the food. They come without contributing anything and then take home all of the leftovers (which they actually fight over sometimes). They lie around and watch TV until it's time to go home. They don't talk to my kids or me. In fact, they couldn't care less about anything that is happening with my family. Did I also mention that my brother-in-law and his wife guilt my husband into helping financially every month?

After 20 years of this, I can't stand the sight of them. Knowing that I have to be cordial and expend all of my energy cooking for them spoils my whole holiday season. I just want to run away, but my kids love Christmas with the family. Help me. How do I cope? I want to have a nice Christmas, not one that is filled with anger and resentment. Is there a way to do that, or am I doomed to let them ruin my Christmas?

—*Bah Humbug*

DEAR BAH HUMBUG: I commend your mother for instilling in you the importance of grace, kindness and generosity. But it's hard to feel gracious, kind or generous when you're too busy feeling resentful. So you have two options. You can keep the celebration cozy, with just you, your husband and your children. There is nothing wrong with doing this, and I encourage you to give it a shot.

If you can't bring yourself to change your plans, then change your attitude. Channel the Whoville spirit. Make your mind up to have a delightful time no matter how frightful your in-laws' behavior. The main takeaway here is that whether or not your holiday is "doomed" is entirely up to you.

Controlling Family Events

DEAR ANNIE: We are a large group of middle-aged siblings with one sister who has little engagement outside the home. She is an empty nester who does not work, volunteer or have any regular friends or social activities.

Our problem occurs when it comes time for a family function. She wants to control the event to the point that we cannot enjoy it. The importance of these events to her self-worth is truly disturbing. She once commandeered a small retirement party, and we received 60 texts and calls within 24 hours. We have regained some ground by politely initiating plans before she does, hosting events at our own homes or avoiding her during events if she's in one of her controlling moods.

Unfortunately, this loss of total control has brought out some mean-spiritedness in her. She will "sweetly" insult or command us in front of relatives, withhold information and find ways to demonstrate that the plans of others are "wrong."

We love our sister, and we know she needs help. We are not comfortable approaching her husband, as their dynamics may be a small part of the problem. We approached our parents, but she behaves well with the older generation, and they don't see what we see. I have given her names of counselors and suggestions for outside activities that don't involve family. The problem is getting worse, and she is turning Machiavellian on us. Any other ideas?

—*Family Exercise in Futility*

DEAR FAMILY: Idle hands are the devil's workshop, especially when they're holding a smartphone. In this case, the "devil" is your sister's pathological need for control, which she has allowed to totally consume her.

Give her a chore so she feels like a part of the plan— something that will satisfy her need to feel needed without making a mess of the whole event.

You've taken many steps to try to help, and I commend your efforts. Let's hope she will be open to seeking help in the future. But at a certain point, you have to accept that you can't control the control freak.

Hatred and Disgust for Stepson

DEAR ANNIE: I am a 42-year-old man with two teenage sons. I have been married to my second wife for almost a year. She has an 11-year-old son, "Brice."

Brice never had a man in his life until I married his mom. He is respectful and a sweet kid, but for some reason, I hate him. I know that sounds harsh, and I am actually ashamed at how I feel, but I cannot seem to warm up to him.

My sons are 14 and 16. They are your typical rough-and-tumble boys. They are into sports, girls and cars. I suppose I am used to that behavior in boys. Brice, on the other hand, is extremely effeminate and sensitive. He would rather be inside reading a book or helping his mom in the kitchen. I came home from work the other day, and he was in an apron helping her bake cookies. I could barely look at him.

I have tried numerous times to get him interested in the things most boys his age are doing, such as playing catch in the backyard. He cries and complains and says how much he hates sports.

My sons have also tried to get him to do things with them, but he will complain the entire time that he hates the outdoors. They pretty much have given up on him. They say he is a whiner and a crybaby.

If I am out somewhere with him and I run into a friend or co-worker, I am actually embarrassed to introduce him as my stepson because of how he acts.

I want to make this very clear: I keep my feelings to myself. I pretend to be a loving parent. But I don't feel any love for him at all. My wife has no clue I feel this way. She always tells me what a wonderful dad I have been to her son.

I know I need counseling or something, but I am too ashamed to talk to anyone and admit I feel what I feel. Is there anything you can suggest?

—Ashamed and Terrible Stepdad

DEAR ASHAMED AND TERRIBLE STEPDAD: Many people believe that if you feel that you hate someone, you actually hate something about yourself that you recognize in the other person. That could be the case here. Perhaps when you were a child, an adult made you feel bad about some aspect of your personality that wasn't stereotypically masculine. Whatever the source of these feelings, a counselor could help you work through them and past them, confidentially and without judgment. That is a counselor's job. You don't need to tell anyone why you're going to counseling—but you do need to go, for your sake and for Brice's. Children pick up on feelings.

Mommy Doesn't Know Best

DEAR ANNIE: I am currently unemployed and living with my parents. Because I have a disability, I am unable to do many of the jobs available locally. Besides my family, I am currently working with several people at the local Department of Labor to find a job related to my degrees— one that will help me start a career. My family wants me to get any job.

One of the local nursing homes has several openings for certified nursing assistants. With the exception of my parents, no one sees this as a good fit for me. After all, my mother is on the nursing home's board. As a result, I'm sure that I would hear about every mistake I made during dinner if I got the job.

My mother is so obsessed with my applying. She asks me several times every day whether I have completed the forms. I'm losing it. I don't know how long it will be before I crack. What should I do?

—Going Nuts

DEAR GOING NUTS: I gather Mom is a wee bit on the overbearing side. Your circumstances might mean you have to live with her, but that doesn't mean you have to live for her. Stand up to her and find your own career. The time out of the house, building your own life, will be invaluable to your sanity.

In the Middle of a Feud

DEAR ANNIE: Last summer, my granddaughter "Emily" got married. Her mother, "Angie" (my daughter), lives in the same town as Emily and said I could stay with her while I was in town. About a week before the wedding, Angie and Emily had a big falling-out. Emily told me she wasn't allowing Angie to come to the wedding.

I talked to Emily for a long time and persuaded her to let her mother and stepfather attend the wedding. On the day of the wedding, we were not seated where the bride's family was supposed to sit. We had to sit a row back, as a symbolic gesture. Then my granddaughter had the best man come and get me and take me back to the dressing room. She asked me whether I would sit in the family section. We discussed this for a while, and I finally said OK. I was taken back into the chapel and seated in the front row, in front of my daughter and the rest of the family.

When the service was over, Angie and her husband were not allowed to go to the reception, so I didn't go, either. When we got back to Angie's home, she wouldn't even talk to me. My son-in-law told me it would probably be better if I went and spent the night elsewhere. I tried to explain why I had sat where I did, but Angie wouldn't even listen to anything I said. She has not spoken to me or answered any letters I have sent her since. I've apologized many times, but she refuses to talk.

I love my daughter very much, but I also love my granddaughter. I was trying to do what I thought was right by them both. My granddaughter talks to me all the time, but my daughter won't have anything to do with me. How can this be resolved so that my daughter and I can be on good terms again? I am 79 years old, and my daughter is 60

—*Heartbroken Mother and Grandmother*

DEAR HEARTBROKEN MOTHER AND GRANDMOTHER: You didn't cause this problem, and you can't fix it. It can be resolved only when your daughter decides to stop being vindictive. She is using you as an emotional punching bag because of the issues she's having with her own daughter.

What you've done so far—explaining your side of the story, expressing your love—is more than enough. Now all you can do is hope she drops the attitude. In the meantime, do keep up your relationship with your granddaughter, but be careful that she's not using you to upset her mom. Don't be a pawn in this petty game.

Who's the Idiot?

DEAR ANNIE: My soon-to-be mother-in-law and I are in an

all-out war via social media. It all started when she posted an article about politics that was full of blatant lies and misinformation. I commented with a few links so she could do further research and see that she was totally wrong. She replied by saying that I am young and naive and my sources were biased. I doubt she even actually read them.

We went back and forth all day, and eventually I told her that she is an idiot if she truly believes what she was saying. She told me to talk to her again when I am ready to grow up. This was about two weeks ago.

My fiancée, "Becky," is not happy with me, to put it mildly. While she doesn't agree with her mom, she's furious that I would be so disrespectful. I feel that her mom was the first one to be disrespectful, by telling me I'm naive.

Becky wants me to call her mom and apologize, but I'm still so annoyed with this woman. On principle, I refuse to do it. I wasn't wrong, and I'm not backing down. I know you have to choose your battles, but I think this one is worth fighting. Annie, what do you think?

—*In the Doghouse*

DEAR DOGHOUSE: I'm not one for name-calling, but I will say that if there's an idiot in this scenario, your future mother-in-law isn't it. You're not winning any battles, just losing the respect of your future in-laws. That's not to mention all the strain you're putting on your fiancée. If you want to debate politics, join a forum or call your representative or yell at the TV; do whatever it takes to get it out of your system. Just don't do it with your partner's family.

Taking the Wheels

DEAR ANNIE: I am at a loss as to how to get my car back from my mom's house. A little history first: My brother and his family have lived at my parents' home on and off since they got married because of financial hardship. I have also lived there at times during my adult life, but I have some physical and mental health issues that preclude my living by myself. And when I did live there, I paid my way. I bought groceries, paid the cable bill or paid for whatever else my folks asked me to.

Anyway, I have always had a car. I have made the car payments and the insurance payments and had "custody" of my car except when I have been physically unable to drive. (I have epilepsy, and the state won't let you drive for six months after a seizure.)

A few months ago, I had to move out of my parents' house and in with my sister for my sanity and space. My brother asked whether he could borrow my car for a few days until he could get his fixed. I said yes, but I let him know that I needed it back after a few days for my own needs. Then my mom started to ask for him, and it has evolved into a situation in which I have had my car for about nine or 10 days out of the past 30. He was supposed to use his bonus check to fix his car but didn't.

Right now, my brother is keeping my car. He argues that our mom is 80 and his wife is extremely ill and they need it in case of an emergency. What am I supposed to do in an emergency? Am I asking too much to have the car I am paying for?

—*Between a Rock and a Junk Car*

DEAR BETWEEN A ROCK AND A JUNK CAR: You've made my job easy. No, you are not asking too much to have the car you are paying for. I think that at this point, you need to stop asking. Simply tell them. You will be going there to retrieve your car. End of discussion.

Gifts Cause for Discomfort

DEAR ANNIE: My 94-year-old mother has had a sweetheart for about eight years. "John" is 97, is almost blind and deaf, depends heavily on his walker and has begun showing signs of mental confusion. His two sons care for him. Their circumstances appear to be modest.

John is smitten with my mom and has recently started giving her money. First it was $70, which she used to buy some blouses; then it was $100, "for pants." Yesterday, he gave her $200. (I have not been present during these interactions, but Mom has shown me the money.) John insists that these gifts must be kept secret from his sons.

I am uncomfortable with keeping the secret and the money and am afraid there will be more coming down the pike. I do not want to betray his trust by telling his sons. My concerns are that this may be money that the family needs, that sneaking money to my mom creates an unhealthy atmosphere and that John may not be able-minded enough to make such decisions. Mom does not want the money, but John is insistent. What do you think?

—*Concerned Daughter*

DEAR CONCERNED DAUGHTER: For John, this isn't about the gifts; it's about the giving. He wants his partner to feel cherished. So perhaps your mom could let her benevolent beau know all the ways he makes her feel special that don't involve money. He'll rely less on material things to express his love if he realizes that simply holding her hand makes her feel like a million bucks.

Victim of Family Gossipers

DEAR ANNIE: My husband has a large family. For the past 20 years, we have attended all the family gatherings. A few months ago, we found out my husband's two brothers and their wives have been gossiping about me.

We saw the conversations by accident. Apparently, these two couples get together quite often, and it seems I'm the main topic of conversation. They were basically stalking me on Facebook and monitoring my posts.

All the conversations would go like this: "Did you see what Emily said about how she had to go to the hospital?" "Did you see what Emily said about how she has faith in God?" This went on and on. Every word I said was analyzed and mocked.

Needless to say, I immediately blocked all of them on Facebook, and I no longer post anything personal. But now the problem remains that I don't care to see these people anymore. I have forgiven them, but I would be uncomfortable being in the same room with them, knowing somehow I'd be giving them more fuel for the gossip fire.

My husband is angry about this situation, too, but at the same time, he doesn't want to disappear off the portion of the earth that his family populates. I've had people advise me to take the high road and go to the gatherings and not worry about what they think of me. But I feel too uncomfortable to do that.

I guess my question is: Do I have the right to go invisible? Because that's what I want to do. I have plenty of family and friends to spend the holidays with who love me

—Betrayed

DEAR BETRAYED: If anyone should be practicing a disappearing act, it's your gossiping in-laws. They ought to be ashamed of themselves. But avoidance isn't the answer here. Have your husband talk to his family members about how their gossiping has hurt you. Let's hope that given the chance, they'll apologize and use this as a moment to reflect, because their gossiping says far more about them than it does about you. As Eleanor Roosevelt said, "great minds discuss ideas; average minds discuss events; small minds discuss people."

Grandma Feels Used

DEAR ANNIE: I'm a grandmother to five children. My son Brian and his wife, Amanda, have a 3-year-old and a 6-month-old together.

They live several states away, about a five-hour drive. I get to see them close to once a month, though, as they continually ask me to watch the kids while they go on vacation.

When their baby was only 3 months old, they took a trip to a resort in Mexico. Personally, I would never leave an infant, so I don't understand their desire to leave so often. Now they're going on a weeklong cruise, and I'll be baby-sitting again.

I don't mind watching the grandkids. I love them to the moon and back, and really, I appreciate how nice it is that I get to spend time with them, especially while they're still little and thrilled to see their grandma. But I think it's getting out of hand, and I feel as if my son and daughter-in-law think I don't have a life of my own. Am I being ridiculous?

—*Frustrated Grandma*

Dear Frustrated: Here's a word that will change your life: "No." Try using it the next time your son and his wife are daydreaming of making a tropical getaway and leaving you in charge of their home life.

Giving in to their requests all the time will leave you feeling taken advantage of and resentful. And that's a surefire way to damage your relationship with your son. Set boundaries.

Grieving Mom Alienates Family

DEAR ANNIE: I have never written to an advice columnist before, so please bear with me.

My dad passed away in January 2016 from a tragic motorcycle accident. A driver wasn't paying any attention and hit my dad. He died a week later in the hospital from his injuries. I got the call he passed on the morning of my 40th birthday. It's been a year now, and my mom is still heartbroken. I realize people grieve in their own ways, and seeing as they would have been married for 50 years last June, I can understand that it will take time to heal.

However, what I need help with is this: She has turned bitter and hateful toward everyone. My younger sister and I are married and have families of our own. So Mom feels abandoned when we can't come over every day. I have invited her to places, but she always cancels. She has alienated all her friends, including her best friend of 10 years.

Now she has moved on to my husband and my youngest daughter. She blames my husband for my not spending more time with her.

Last summer, we went on a Colorado vacation, and he wanted it to be just he, our two daughters and I. Mom took that to mean that he feels she isn't a part of our family—which isn't true. I go over there every week, and she refuses to get out of bed, giving one excuse or another. It's come to the point that I have started lying to her about my work hours just so I don't have to put myself in a situation of being disappointed anymore. She has started in on my youngest and says nasty things to my daughter's face, such as, "You're a waste of space." My daughter is 12, and that really hurts her self-esteem. That is the last straw. I love my mom, but attacking my daughter and my husband is unforgivable.

Please, any advice you could give me would be greatly appreciated

—One Foot Out the Door

DEAR ONE: No matter how much your mother might be pushing people away, her behavior sounds like a cry for help.

First, it's important that you not return her bitterness in kind. When she hurls nasty insults at you, simply tell her, "I'm sorry you feel that way." She'll be less inclined to lash out at you once she stops getting the response she's looking for.

Second, emphasize that you'll always love her unconditionally, but if you're going to be part of each other's life, she must find a therapeutic outlet for her grief, whether it's counseling, a support group or a religious adviser. Visit the sites of GriefShare and Soaring Spirits International for more resources.

And no matter what, don't feel guilty for healing. Continue taking vacations with your husband and children. Your mother's grief cannot hold your joy hostage.

Look Who Dropped In

DEAR ANNIE: I occasionally have lunch with a relative whose company I enjoy. We usually have a nice time, but lately she has been bringing a last-minute guest with her without telling me. Sometimes it is another relative, and sometimes it is a person I've never met. This has caused seating confusion and a less desirable room at places where we have reservations. Does this mean she doesn't care for my company, or is it just a lack of manners?

—*Mystified in Michigan*

DEAR MYSTIFIED: I can't divine this woman's reasons. Perhaps she's trying to save time by consolidating her lunch dates (which, I agree, would be bad manners). But there's no need to consult a crystal ball. The next time you're making plans and wondering whether she'll invite anyone else, just ask.

Mom Shocked by Son's Opinion of Her

DEAR ANNIE: Just the other day, my son, "Ben," was talking to his stepdad, and he said some hurtful things about me—that I'm all about me, that it's always my way or the highway. I took that very personally. It made me cry.

I never expected my eldest son to say something or feel that way about me. I took it as him trying to hurt my feelings. He needs to understand that with the kids all out of the house now, I do often feel that it is all about me. The house is empty; my two elder kids don't even call me to see whether I'm OK or sick, and I think that if I ever become sick, I will keep it to myself and not inform them. Am I wrong for that?

Now I don't feel comfortable even asking to see my grandchildren, because I fear it's been embedded in their minds that Grandma is all about her and no one else.

I posted about this situation on Facebook to see how

everyone would respond and what advice people might offer. A co-worker came to me and comforted me about the situation. All I could do was cry. I never knew my kids felt that way about their mom. Please give me some advice

—*Devastated Mom*

DEAR DEVASTATED MOM: Slow down and take a deep breath. This is a whirlwind, but it seems that at the center of it all is your feeling of abandonment. I reckon that's caused you to lash out in ways you might not recognize as lashing out—with guilt trips, for instance. If you've been trying to get your kids to pay attention to you by making them feel bad, that has backfired. It's time to stop catastrophizing and start communicating. Talk to your children. Tell them you didn't realize how negatively they felt about your behavior. Ask what you could do to be a bigger part of their lives. And for everyone's sake, please stop posting about it on Facebook.

Enabling a Self-Destructive Son

DEAR ANNIE: My stepson, "Dale," lives off benefits from the government and his father—my sweet, loving husband, who is in his 70s. Dale has not worked for five years, and his dad bails him out of every scrape and crisis he gets himself into. Dale has been fired from every job he has ever had. He has spent time in rehab. He lies, steals, is involved in risky behavior and may be back on drugs. The final straw is that his landlord has kicked him out.

There is a history of depression, and he is on medication, but physically he is fit and able. As a couple, we have attended National Alliance on Mental Illness meetings (a great organization) and ongoing marriage guidance sessions to try to agree on boundaries, etc., when dealing with this situation.

A parent always loves his kids, but when is it time to say "enough is enough" and let them go? I will not have Dale come and live with us in our tiny home. The real problem is that my husband is Dale's enabler. When will my husband wake up and accept that he is being taken in, lied to and manipulated on almost a daily basis? My husband's view remains, "What if I don't do enough and he harms himself?" My husband needs to give himself permission to say, "I tried!"

—*Frustrated Stepmother*

DEAR FRUSTRATED STEPMOTHER: I agree that your husband needs to give himself permission to detach with love. But your husband must decide this for himself, just as Dale must decide for himself that he needs help. Attempting to rush your husband to this realization won't help—and in fact might backfire.

I'm so glad you're both in therapy and attending NAMI meetings. I would also urge you to attend a 12-step family program, such as Families Anonymous, Nar-Anon or Al-Anon. Hearing how others have learned to put the focus back on themselves might inspire you and your husband to do the same.

Grandpa Knows Best

DEAR ANNIE: Our 39-year-old son is married with three children. Ever since he got married, he has been dealing with overbearing and intrusive in-laws.

My son and daughter-in-law were house hunting a few years ago, and there was a home going up for auction they wanted to check out. They mentioned it in her parents' company. Before the auction took place, her father, "Steve," had purchased the home for them to live in.

They might not have purchased the house after seeing it, as it was termite-infested, had no working fireplaces and had a roof that needed replacing. They used the money they made selling their previous home for upgrades for this home. Steve would not allow them to secure a loan for the home to pay him back, so the house remains in his name.

Our son has a job with which he can support his family, a great head on his shoulders to make great family decisions and good credit, so he can get loans at the bank on his own without any help. His wife goes along with whatever her parents say or want her to do.

It is causing strife in our son's marriage, plus it's putting strain on our relationship with our daughter-in-law, and on some occasions, we have not been allowed to visit. My husband and I support a loving family relationship, and when asked for advice on family matters, we give it. But we do not interfere to her parents' degree, because neither of us was raised that way.

The issue now is that our son's job is relocating him to a different state. His employer will allow him time to visit his new job location and look for housing. My son secured a Realtor in the area to start the house-hunting process. My daughter-in-law started looking online at homes in this city. She found a home that she liked online and told my son she wanted it because it had all the right amenities. He insisted that they wait till they could look at the houses in person and find one that really met all their needs (e.g., a good school district for the children).

Our son notified us today that Steve purchased the home our daughter-in-law found online, sight unseen, for them to live in. This behavior is not allowing our son to be a husband, partner in decision-making and father to his children. Steve grants all of his daughter's wishes. We want to support our son because we know he is hurting. What advice would you recommend we give him in this troubling time?

—*Concerned Parents*

DEAR CONCERNED: Wow. I had to pick my jaw up off the floor a couple of times while reading your letter. I can't imagine what Steve's financial situation must be like, to give away houses like candy. But I digress.

You're right that this Daddy-to-the-rescue dynamic is not conducive to a healthy marriage. But from the sound of it, your son hasn't expressed any of these frustrations to his wife. That lack of communication is even more toxic than intrusive in-laws. Marriage counseling would offer him a safe space to express his feelings to his wife. And given that she's grown up thinking her dad's behavior is normal, it might take an objective third party to help her see that it's not.

The Other Grandma

DEAR ANNIE: I'm quite sure there are others in my shoes. I have a 9-year-old grandson, "Bradley." He has been in and out of our lives, mainly because of the fact that his mother, "Jill," and my son, "Andrew," are not married and my son is not to have custody of Bradley at all. Jill and Bradley have mainly lived with Jill's parents. We have never been as close as grandparents and grandson should be, but my husband, my daughters and I have tried. I knew this, but his mother finally admitted that one of the reasons she never left him at my house while she ran errands or let him spend the night was that her dad didn't want him around us. She said her dad (Bradley's grandpa) was always worried that we'd let Andrew come over and kidnap him—which we would never do.

Anyway, for about a year now, when Bradley does come over, he never talks unless we talk first, and even then he only has one- or two-word answers. Jill has always let him sit in on adult conversations, something I totally disagree with. If she starts talking about how this or that is going wrong in her life, he jumps in and makes sure to give his input, but it's adult stuff he doesn't need to know about. We realize he forms his opinions based on what his mother says.

Jill generally only brings him around during holidays, when gifts are in order. We can tell he really doesn't want to be here but his mother is forcing him to come to get a present. My dilemma: Do I continue buying gifts for him in the amount that I do for my other grandchildren, the ones I see often? Am I supposed to overlook what Jill is doing and pretend that he is doing nothing wrong? I don't want to be the grandma who is trying to gift a grandson into coming more, because that has no effect on him anyway.

—*Christmas in Kentucky*

DEAR CHRISTMAS IN KENTUCKY: This little boy is only 9, and based on your letter, he's probably getting a lot of mixed signals from the adults in his life about how to behave and whom he can trust. It's no wonder he's a little reserved.

You're under no obligation to buy him gifts of a certain value, but I would continue to show him the same love and attention you show your other grandchildren. If his home life is chaotic, your reliable support could mean more than you know.

Back to Work After Having a Baby

DEAR ANNIE: My husband and I welcomed a beautiful baby girl into the world three months ago. She's our first child and the love of our lives. I was blessed with 12 weeks' leave from work after she was born, and I cherished that time immensely. I've now returned to work and been back for two weeks. The first day was difficult. I cried several times but eventually got back into the groove of working life. Everyone kept telling me that returning to work would get easier.

Yesterday, my husband texted me to let me know our daughter had rolled over for the first time. I was so proud! But then the sadness kicked in. I wasn't there to see it. This morning, I woke up late. I overslept by almost an hour. I had just enough time to pump and get a quick shower before having to run out the door to go to work. I missed out on the precious time I have in the morning when it's just my daughter and I while she nurses.

I've always considered myself a strong woman, one who can take on whatever difficulties life throws her way. Returning to work is one obstacle I'm not sure I'm strong enough to take on. All I can think about is how many more "firsts" I'm going to potentially miss. How do working moms do it? How do you balance work and wanting to be there for your child? Not working isn't financially an option for my family, but working is causing emotional and mental stress for me. When does it get easier?

—*Heartbroken Mom*

DEAR HEARTBROKEN: I understand where you are coming from. What strikes me about your letter is how much you appreciate the time that you have with your daughter. I have found that the quality of time you spend with your children can be more important than the quantity. Perhaps you could ask your boss about the possibility of working from home one or two days a week. Many companies today are flexible and understanding on this issue.

And be sure to ask your husband to send plenty of photos and videos, especially documenting every milestone. Hang in there. It really will get easier.

Stiffed on a Birthday

DEAR ANNIE: What should I do about my adult children's birthdays? My birthday is Jan. 1. Most years, my children acknowledge it with a card, not just a text. This year, all I got were texts from them. I was very hurt.

Their father's birthday is later in the year, and they will buy him a gift plus a card.

May I just text them on their birthdays to reciprocate their behavior? Their father won't remember to get a card, etc. I feel like giving to charities in their names for their birthdays. Would that be OK? I'm in a pickle regarding what to do

—*Birthday Blues*

DEAR BIRTHDAY: First, happy belated birthday. And shame on your children. The least they could have done was send a card. I'm guessing you're such a giver that they take dear old Mom for granted. Perhaps they need to be reminded that you have feelings. Tell them—or have your husband tell them—that their actions (or lack thereof) hurt you.

As for what to do for their birthdays, giving to charity is always a great idea. Go for it. I dare them to complain.

Adventures With Social Media

DEAR ANNIE: In this day and age, it is very hard to ignore what people are doing in their private lives when it's plastered all over Facebook, Instagram and Twitter. Specifically, I am referring to photos of social gatherings that have me feeling left out.

I have a grown child who is married. Recently, the married couple moved. When they moved in to their home, we were there to physically help them. The whole family helped in their move—all four parents, an uncle, a sibling and a nephew. We also gave them a very generous check for a housewarming gift so they could buy a few extra things for their new home.

It has been my great displeasure to learn, from their posts on Facebook, that my son and daughter-in-law have hosted a few dinners in their new home. She's had a "girls' night in," and he's had a "guys' night in." They've hosted a dinner party for my daughter-in-law's side of the family. However, as parents of the other child in that marriage, we have yet to be invited to their new home for a social gathering.

I am trying not to take this personally, but I can't help but feel slighted and disappointed that our family has yet to be invited to their home. I "like" all the pictures from all their parties, but inside I'm bothered that we aren't important enough to have been invited over as everyone else has been. Suggestions? Thoughts?

—Family Matters

DEAR FAMILY MATTERS: I can tell your feelings are about to boil over, so turn down the flame or take off the lid.

The former means cooling off. They only moved in recently, as you said; maybe they wanted to host an intimate dinner with each side of the family separately and your daughter-in-law's side just happened to be first. The latter means expressing how you feel—but in a healthy, positive way, free of guilt-tripping and accusations. For example, you might tell your son, "We'd love to come over sometime when you're settled in and it's convenient for you." The main point is not to blow up.

Election Arguments

DEAR ANNIE: I'll try to keep this nonpartisan and just give you the bare essentials. My sister and I are both in our late 50s. She's only two years younger than I am, and we grew up extremely close. We went to college together and made sure never to move too far away from each other or our parents afterward.

But she is a member of one major political party, and I'm a member of the other one. The presidential election caused a big strain on our relationship. I thought things would get better after Election Day, but they've gotten even worse. She's unwilling to compromise and see my point of view, and to be honest, I can't see her point of view, either.

Before the campaign season started, we talked on the phone at least three times a week. Now we haven't talked in two weeks, and I'm worried the distance between us will just continue to grow. I keep thinking I should swallow my pride and tell her she's right on a few points (even though I don't believe it) just to smooth things over. But I can't bring myself to do it. Will we ever be as close as we were?

—*Family Divided*

DEAR FAMILY: This election has done a number on many families. Based on what I've heard from other readers, the disagreement you and your sister are having is happening at tables all across the nation.

It's entirely possible—healthy, even—to love someone who has different opinions. You eliminate a lot of frustration once you realize that yelling never changed anybody's mind. Embrace the relief that comes with agreeing to disagree.

That said, I'm sure that if you two made a list of all the things you have in common, it would be much longer than the list of all the things you don't. You're just obsessing over the latter. Remember: You were sisters long before you even knew what a Democrat or Republican is. Give her a call today, and talk about your children, your health, a good book you're reading—anything but politics.

Hearts Will Break

DEAR ANNIE: I am the father of two married girls, who both have made bad decisions on spouses—one in her first marriage and the other in her second marriage. In light of this, it concerns me that I did not ever vet my daughters' choices of men.

Now that I have five granddaughters, two of whom are twins and madly in love with boyfriends, I feel I should be looking out for them—or at least encouraging them to make good decisions. These twins are in their early 20s. One side of my brain tells me to stay out of it, but the other side doesn't want them to get hurt in any way. Both of these men come from good parents and families; however, I would like to get to know their beliefs and ideas about marriage and family life. How do I do this without seeming to be a nosy old man? (I am a young 73.) I love my grandkids. I just don't ever want their hearts to be broken.

Which road do I take, knowing I will never get a redo?

—*Grandpa B*

DEAR GRANDPA: The bad news: At some point, your granddaughters' hearts probably will be broken. But that's part of growing up; it's an opportunity to learn and become a stronger person, and you would be doing them a disservice to deny them the chance. And besides, you couldn't prevent it even if you tried. The heart is an experiential learner.

So my advice would be to keep an ongoing friendship with your granddaughters. Give them the necessary tools to make good decisions. Encourage them to trust their instincts. Listen to them; offer your wisdom when they seek it. Lead by example in the way you treat their grandmother and your daughters. And when those mistakes and heartaches inevitably come, help them to learn as best they can from the experience. Though life is ultimately the teacher of its most important lessons, you can serve as a trusted tutor.

A Sister's Insult on a Social Network

DEAR ANNIE: Recently, I copied an article and reposted it on Facebook. The article dealt with a woman who has handicapped license plates. She does not appear to be physically handicapped, although she is. Another woman had approached her in a parking lot and harassed her for using the handicapped parking spot. The gist of the article was to not pass judgment on people and make assumptions.

When I posted it, I added a disclaimer in the comments area to let people know that I wasn't the original author. I also commented that my husband has a handicapped placard but does not look handicapped and that if someone did approach us negatively, I would be ticked.

My sister commented on this post and said, "You are an idiot."

I am hurt, and I'm angry with her. I don't understand why she would make a comment such as this to her own sister on social media where my children, grandchildren and friends can see. I deleted the post and unfriended her. Did I go too far?

—*Hurt Sister*

DEAR HURT: Using social media to settle disputes between family members or friends is like trying to repair reading glasses with a sledgehammer; you have a blunt tool and an incredibly delicate object, and it results in a totally unnecessary broken mess.

Your sister is squarely in the wrong here, and I understand why you unfriended her. But that is not a long-term real-world solution. Because her comment seemed to you to come totally out of the blue, you two must be on very different pages. Talk to her in person if you can or on the phone if not. Ask her what she was thinking. Communication is the key here—real communication, between two sisters, not two screens.

Sister Still Single

DEAR ANNIE: My younger sister is a 59-year-old woman

who has never been married. She's fun, creative and full of life, and she still has her looks. I also know she's really lonely. After a string of bad boyfriends in her 20s and 30s, she gave up on dating and has since devoted almost all her energy to her work and her pets.

She's gone on a few dates here and there over the years, but she refuses to do any kind of online dating because she thinks that it's "desperate" and that "only freaks are out online." She refuses to hear me when I say otherwise. Every time I try to approach the subject of dating, she tells me that I have no idea what I'm talking about and that we're too different to understand each other.

And that's true. We were never close growing up. She was the "wild child" who dropped out of high school, and I was the "good daughter" who got a college degree. And there's a 10-year age difference. Also, I have been married for more than 30 years and have two great kids. I feel guilty and like a braggart every time I talk about my family. And her resentment has only grown after the recent death of her pet. How do I help my sister find someone when she doesn't want to hear it? Maybe she'll listen to you

—Elder Sister in Omaha

DEAR ELDER SIS: A white picket fence and 2 1/2 kids are not for everyone. Plenty of people live amazingly fulfilled lives without getting married and having children.

I don't think your sister would be "full of life," "creative" and attractive if she were lonely and miserable. Once you stop forcing your idea of happiness on her, that guilt you mentioned may magically disappear.

You Owe Me, Mom and Dad

DEAR ANNIE: My husband and I have two children, one adopted at birth and the other born to us later. Our adopted child never attended college because of unfortunate choices he made in his teens. Trouble with the law followed, but he was able to pick up a GED while incarcerated.

Our second child had no problems growing up and so was on track to attend college—which we paid for, except for a Stafford loan she applied for each year. Our son has come through his early troubles (we never abandoned him) and has his own manual labor business.

Now to our problem: Do we owe both children money to launch them on their careers?

Our son believes we owe him money now to help him build up his business, as his sister received an education (some years ago) to help her in her professional life. I'm not sure what's going on, but he went on a tirade recently, castigating us for overlooking his needs, etc., and asking why he was adopted, saying he would have done better with his natural parents. We are now many years past being able to help him substantially in his business needs, as my husband and I have been retired for about nine years and live on a fixed income

—Mom and Dad

DEAR MOM AND DAD: Just because you helped your daughter through college does not mean you retroactively "owe" your son an equivalent amount, and the fact that he is demanding as much makes this clear: The only thing you owe him is a fat stack of tough love.

Our job as parents is to do everything we can to support our children and give them strong foundations while they're under our care. It sounds as if you did as much of that as you could.

And now he is trying every technique in the guilt tripper's handbook to push your buttons and get what he wants. It's manipulative and selfish. To fold would only reinforce this attitude.

Your son is an adult now, and he has the ability to make money and apply for loans on his own. It's time to help him spread his wings, whether he wants to or not.

The Forgotten Side of the Family

DEAR ANNIE: I am writing because another Mother's Day will soon be upon us and, once again, my grown stepchildren—who were grown and on their own when their parents divorced—will ignore me.

Every year, they celebrate Mother's Day without thinking of me at all. That wouldn't hurt so much if I could write it off as just my being a stepparent—but every Father's Day, they include their stepfather in the celebration.

Many other times, they share with their mother and stepfather whatever news they have—a new vehicle they bought, the name of their unborn baby, etc. Their father and

I do eventually learn most news, but it's usually long after the fact. We all get along, and there is absolutely no animosity at all among any of us; we love them, and we both love the former in-laws.

All I ask is for them to treat their father as well as they treat their stepfather. I hope that they see themselves in this letter and do a gut check. Their father loves them very much, but he is accustomed to not being included, so he hides his pain from them.

Since we married, he has leaned more on me, seeing as they don't ever call him just to chat. I call my dad regularly, and my husband was astounded when he learned that. I hurt for him and for them because they have no idea how they hurt us, and we will never let them know.

Is it asking too much to be included in their news? We share our news with them and don't leave them out, as far as I can tell. They are very family-oriented, just not with their dad

—*Midwestern Stepmother Loving Them From the Outside*

DEAR MIDWESTERN: The sentence that most struck me in your letter was this: "They have no idea how they hurt us, and we will never let them know." Your husband hides his pain from them, so for all they know, he's fine with talking only once in a while. They may even think he prefers it that way. This is the status quo they're used to, and until you take the initiative to call more and speak up about your wish to be included, your stepchildren will continue in their current pattern. So shake up the routine. Call them often. Invite them to visit, and go visit them. Let them know how much you value the time together.

Annie Lane

Declining Relationship With Daughter

DEAR ANNIE: My ex-husband was emotionally, verbally and physically abusive, and he was a womanizer from the very beginning. So I divorced him in the 1980s; I then kept custody of our daughter.

All was good between my daughter and me for 10 years— before my ex managed to work his way back into my life with his usual charm. I really thought he had changed. What's that old saying about a leopard?

I have to confess that we both drank a lot. But I seemed to be the only one at fault for everything. His abuse got worse and worse over the years. He did and said anything to destroy my self-esteem and credibility with my friends and even my co-workers. He managed to destroy my relationship with my daughter, too.

They started to hang out in the bars together, and she started to treat me just as he did. They planned for weeks to throw me out when I temporarily lost my job, and they tried to hurt me in other ways. They would huddle in corners of bars together, kissing as if they were lovers, watching my reactions to their behavior. I had people ask me whether they were actually sleeping together, and to be honest, I wasn't really sure.

It came to a head one night when she was getting ready to go out with her dad again while I was sleeping. She was going to leave her 18-month-old son with me without even letting me know I was baby-sitting. I woke up before she left

105

and was very angry when I figured it out. I woke the child up and told him Mommy was going bye-bye and asked whether he wanted to go with her. At this point, she hit me and knocked me down. Before I could get up, she hit me again. Then she called her dad, and he told me to get out, which I did. I went back to work shortly after this, thank goodness, but they left me with nothing financially. I had to start all over again.

To this day, my daughter has never apologized for any of her behavior or actions. Trust me; having your child treat you like a piece of garbage isn't something that's easy to get over. She has also tried to turn everyone she knows against me ever since then, even my current husband. She is doing exactly the same things her father did.

I no longer drink at all, for the record.

I don't know where to go from here. She says she has tried to have a relationship with me, but I just don't see it happening, not with the hatefulness still coming at me.

Should I try to repair the damage that has been done, or should I just walk completely away? If this is her way of showing love, I don't think I want her love anymore.

—Wits' End

DEAR WITS': There is, unfortunately, much more to hash out here than the space of this column allows. But it sounds as if the years of abuse from your ex-husband saddled you with a lot of emotional baggage that you're still carrying today, and I strongly recommend seeing a therapist.

If you're unable to see one in person, consider using BetterHelp or TalkSpace. These websites connect patients with health care professionals via video chats, text messages and phone calls. I hope you and your daughter can build a healthy relationship together over time.

That Wasn't the Deal

DEAR ANNIE: This is not an earthshaking problem, but it concerns me. I am a childless widow and celebrate Christmas with my sister's family, consisting of her adult children and their spouses; her adult grandchildren and their spouses or significant others; and one toddler.

Everyone was buying a gift for everyone else, and the cost became more than some could handle. The Christmas before last, we decided to draw names so no one would have to buy more than one gift.

Last year, I dutifully brought my one gift to the gathering, as did most others. However, it turned out my sister had "cheated" and bought several gifts for each person. Dismayed, the rest of us asked why she had not followed the rules. Her reply was that this was her last chance to give everyone a gift. The whole point had been to relieve the burden on those who aren't well-off.

Annie, I am not wealthy, but I am very capable of giving a small gift to everyone in our family. My joy in the whole exercise is in seeing people's pleasure as they open the gifts. I have no wish or need to receive any gifts. I feel that my sister robbed me of the pleasure of giving, and I feel cheated. I am torn about what to do this holiday.

My natural inclination is to get each person something and let the chips fall where they may, but I don't want it to look as if I'm trying to outdo my sister. I have a feeling she will repeat last year's action. I tried to feel her out, and her response was suspiciously vague. What do you think I should do?

—*Love My Family*

DEAR LOVE: Your sister no doubt lives by the adage, "'Tis better to give than to receive." But the irony is that she's denying her loved ones the gift of feeling generous themselves. She probably hasn't thought of it that way. She may think you all are just begging off the presents out of politeness and would be delighted to receive them. Break out the milk and cookies, and sit her down for a sisterly fireside chat, explaining how the rogue Santa act leaves you feeling robbed.

If she pooh-poohs your concerns and hauls in the toy sack anyway, don't let it steal your Christmas spirit. At the end of the day, she wants to shower her loved ones with presents. You can't fault her too much for that.

You're Worth More Than Your Estate

DEAR ANNIE: I am 90 years old and, considering my age, in fairly good health. My wife of 60 years died seven years ago. Almost all of my wartime buddies are gone, as well as my high-school friends.

I live in relative comfort in a retirement home. My two grown children live far away, but thanks to the internet, we keep in touch almost weekly. Thanks to a rather frugal life and some investments, I have no money problems.

The problem is that as of late, I am obsessed with the thought, which tends to keep me awake at night, that it is my parental duty to die as soon as possible so as not to deplete the inheritance any further. Assisted suicide is out of the question, so that leaves the illegal type. The thought itself does not bother me, as I feel that I have lived a most interesting and exciting life—well above the average—but this is the end. So what do I do?

—To Be or Not to Be

DEAR TBNB: Please, keep being. You've worked hard all your life to be able to live out a comfortable retirement and watch your grandchildren grow. Your purpose in life was never merely to provide financially for your family members; it was to support them in every sense of the word. That's still true now.

Your great example of love, selflessness and a 60-year marriage—that is the inheritance that really matters, the gift you've already given your children and grandchildren. Your presence in their lives means so much more to them than money ever could. Imagine the heartache they would feel to know you took your own life.

If your savings have dwindled by the time you pass away, so what? You are so much greater than the sum of your assets, and I'm sure that if your family members knew you were feeling this way, they would tell you the same thing.

If you find yourself consumed with persistent thoughts of suicide, call the National Suicide Prevention Lifeline at 800-273-8255.

◆

I HAVE A CHRONIC CASE OF FOMO. IS THERE A CURE?

Friendship

The Interesting Lives of Others

DEAR ANNIE: My friends have brought to my attention that I have a chronic case of FOMO (fear of missing out). I have to admit they're right. With social media, I can't help but constantly check what's going on. I have anxiety that I'm not going out enough, not socializing enough and not making enough friends. I keep deleting my social media accounts, but then I cave and reactivate them a few days later.

For instance, I recently went to a concert with my boyfriend. We were having a great time, but then I saw a picture of a lot of my friends at a housewarming party. They looked as if they were having a blast. My boyfriend immediately noticed my expression as I looked at my phone and got angry that I was obsessing over what else was going on again.

My previous boyfriend also complained that I was always on my phone and I seemed to be somewhere else mentally. I know they're right, but I still do it. I can't help but feel anxious that I've missed opportunities. How do you squash this feeling?

—Stereotypical Millennial

DEAR STEREOTYPICAL: Sadly, you're not alone. The fear-of-missing-out plague runs rampant among today's youth. The irony is that FOMO actually makes you miss out on life. The constant anxiety about what you may be missing prevents you from living in the present. Scrolling endlessly through photo feeds on social media, worried there's someplace else you should be, you have no awareness of your surroundings or the people you are with and can actually talk to.

Look into mindfulness meditation, and try taking a break from social media again. There are programs out there (one has the apt name of SelfControl) that allow you to block yourself from accessing certain websites. And keep in mind that everything looks much more fun the way people present it on the internet.

Dirty Dealing

DEAR ANNIE: I am one of a group of guys who have been friends and card players for over 30 years. For the past three decades, I have witnessed one of our players, "Charlie," cheat every time we play, but I've said nothing. When it's his time to deal, he shuffles the cards, looks at them and positions them to his liking so that he will deal what he wants to himself.

I notice this every time, but no one else does. We are all very good friends, and I don't want to make a scene, so I say nothing and keep it to myself, burning inside. If I did bring it up in front of everyone, it could bring an end to our game circle. Plus, I know that Charlie would absolutely deny it, and I would look like a fool.

This cheating pays off for him, because he wins about 80 to

90 percent of the time. How can I handle this without destroying our long-standing card game?

—*Sleight of Hand Observer*

DEAR OBSERVER: If you've managed to keep your feelings on this matter to yourself for 30 years, you must have a phenomenal poker face. It's well past time to flush Charlie's dirty tactics out into the open. The best way to go about this is to talk to one of the other players and ask whether he's noticed anything unusual about the way Charlie deals. After 30 years of playing with this guy, I have a feeling he'll know what you're referring to. But if not, tell him to keep an eye out the next time the group gets together.

Once you've got a witness corroborating your claim, go to the others in your group (minus Charlie) and lay it all on the table. Whoever is closest to Charlie should sit him down privately and let him know the group is wise to his maneuvers. He may still deny it, but he'll be hard-pressed to try it again knowing all eyes are on him.

Cruisin' for a Bruisin'

DEAR ANNIE: Recently, my husband and I made plans to go on a cruise along with three other couples. It was up to each couple to make their own travel plans for getting to the port. My husband and I didn't want to drive into the major city from which the cruise is departing, so we decided we would drive to a nearby town from which a shuttle to the cruise is offered. The shuttle ride takes a couple of hours, but we felt it would be worth avoiding the hassle and cost of parking in the city.

One of the other couples, "Tom" and "Judy," whom we don't know very well, ended up wanting to ride with us. This would have been fine if they just wanted to ride along with us to our original destination. But they expected us to drive them right to the cruise ship! When I told them what our plans were, they kept asking whether it would be too late to change our plans and drive straight to the port instead. When I stood firm, they begrudgingly said they'd ride with our other friends. (They didn't want to ride with them at first because Tom and Judy are both smokers and won't be allowed to smoke in their car. My husband and I aren't smokers but would have let them smoke.)

I think that their asking us to change our plans to accommodate them was really unreasonable. What do you think?

—*Confused Cruiser*

DEAR CONFUSED: I think these two must have started in on the mai tais a little early. You are their acquaintances, not their chauffeurs, and I'm glad you didn't change your plans to suit them.

But when it comes time to shove off, I suggest that you leave the negative baggage at the dock and give this couple another chance. It will make for smoother sailing and a better overall vacation. Bon voyage.

A Friend in Debt

DEAR ANNIE: My wife and I are in a pickle. We are friends with another couple, "Josh" and "Vanessa." Vanessa happens to be a teacher at our kids' school. One day, I was picking up my offspring and started chatting with her. I could tell she was sad and asked her about it. That's when the floodgates opened.

She started telling me how she's racked up credit card debt, and she said Josh doesn't know about it. Josh has been under a lot of stress, and she doesn't want to tell him. I consoled her and asked how much, thinking maybe a few hundred bucks.

Her: "17."

Me: "Thousand?"

Her: (slowly nods)

I lied and told her it's OK. I also told her she has to tell Josh. She agreed and said she's planning on doing it next month, after he's past a deadline at work. Then she asked whether my wife and I would lend her $500 for the time being so she could pay the minimum. I told her we'd talk it over.

So now we've got two questions. First, should we give her the money? Second, if need be, should we tell Josh at some point? If we were to tell him, Vanessa would hate us. But otherwise, Josh would hate us after eventually finding out. What would you do?

—Couple in a Conundrum

DEAR COUPLE: Sit this one out.

Don't give Vanessa the money. Doing so would only enable her to maintain her spending addiction.

Don't talk to Josh. Let Vanessa be the one to tell him. She'll have to do it soon anyway if you don't lend her the money for the credit card minimum.

I know you want to help, but resist. The road to hell is paved with good intentions, and it's got an express lane for people who get in the middle of their friends' relationship problems.

Friend or Tenant?

DEAR ANNIE: My friend bought a condo in Florida. She wants me to come stay for a week while she is there but thinks she needs to charge me $350 to stay with her. Why would a friend need to charge you if she is there, too? If I chip in for some food, what am I paying $350 for? Is this fair?

—*Feeling Used*

DEAR FEELING USED: It does not seem right to me to ask that of a friend. If it were a vacation rental and you were splitting the cost, sure. But this is a condo she owns, and she's invited you to come visit. Perhaps the strain of the cost of the condo was more than she fully realized it would be; that's the only plausible explanation I can think of for her charging a fee. Regardless, treating friends like customers is no way to pay the mortgage. If she is looking to make $350 a week off houseguests, she should open a bed-and-breakfast.

A Rift and a Dying Friend

DEAR ANNIE: My question is urgent and can't wait. I don't know what to do.

My best friend is suffering from a quick and aggressive form of ovarian cancer. We don't know how much longer she has and suspect it won't be long. For more than 25 years, I have talked to her at least four times a week and seen her at least once a week. She has been an active participant in my entire family life and is beloved by my spouse, children and extended family. We are all taking this news extremely hard. The hole in our lives is huge.

About 10 years ago, there was a rumor that she and my husband had a thing. It was small-town jealousy of the fact that the four of us had happy lives. If we had lived anywhere else, it would not have been an issue to have opposite-sex friendships. Small towns where people don't move away focus on anything that seems interesting.

We thought it was all fine, but it now seems her husband never was OK with it. He quit coming around, and we never addressed it. We thought that the reason he declined our invitations was that he was busy working. Now we know he is still uncomfortable with us. She probably didn't tell us because she was embarrassed.

If there were time to be mad, I would be so mad. We would have made it right if we had known he was harboring this type of resentment. We could have made sure everyone was OK. Now she is probably dying, and we aren't there with her.

There was a time when we would have been the people he would have called for any kind of help. We moved the furniture, chopped the trees, patched the driveway, etc. We were the best friends when he needed us to be and out of sight and out of mind the rest of the time, I guess.

How do we fix this before it is too late? He is controlling of time and visitors and not receptive right now. We don't want to go behind his back and want to make this right. This is so heartbreaking to all. The few family members who have been able to see her say she is depressed and so sad about the loss of control of her life and feels trapped and dependent.

I miss my best friend and don't know how to make this better for everyone. What do you suggest to heal this rift I didn't realize was this deep? Don't want my heart to die, too

—Love My Friend

DEAR LOVE: If ever there was a time to heal this rift, it's now. Call her husband. Empathize with the complicated emotions he's no doubt feeling. He may have seized onto this issue as something external on which he could project all his anger over his wife's illness. Whatever his reasons, remind him that a grudge hurts the person holding it. And if he's so attached to the pain that he doesn't want to let go, that's his own prerogative. He can stay angry. But he can't force his wife to be part of that anger.

Implore him, for her sake, to allow you to visit. If he feels uncomfortable, he can leave the house for a few hours while you're there. Ultimately, if you want to see your best friend and she wants to see you, go see her—with or without his permission.

Germy Friends

DEAR ANNIE: Two elderly friends I know who live far away made plans to spend about six days in my city. I invited them to stay at my house for three nights, and they made reservations to stay in a downtown hotel for the rest of their visit. I had not seen them for a number of years, and I thought it would be nice to spend time with them. I thought I would ease their travel burdens by having them stay with me, at least for part of their visit. Traveling when you are 80-plus can sometimes be hard on you.

When I picked them up at the airport, both were sick with a cold. I became very concerned about my own health (and those around me), given that the previous winter, I had a severe cold that turned into pneumonia. It took more than three months for me to get better, even with antibiotics.

They sneezed, coughed and blew their noses the whole time they stayed with me. We were often in close contact, not only inside the house but also in the car, given that I drove them around for sightseeing. To my surprise, they did not seem to be that worried about my getting sick. Unfortunately, I did end up catching their cold and was bedridden for four days after they left.

I don't want to be called a bad host who reneges on a promise. But should I have suggested to them upon their arrival that it would not be wise for them to stay with me, given their health situation? Staying at the same hotel at which they had reservations later in the week might have been an option. We still could have socialized, but it would have minimized my chances of getting sick. Would this suggestion have been too selfish?

—*Still Feeling Sick*

DEAR STILL FEELING SICK: When you have a history of pneumonia or another serious respiratory illness, the sniffles are nothing to sniff at. Yes, it would have been perfectly OK for you to explain your concerns to your friends and ask whether they'd mind checking in to the hotel a few days early.

Fingers crossed all your future houseguests are healthy, but if you find yourself in this situation again, speak up. Though your friends may have recovered from their colds, they'd feel pretty crummy if they knew they got you sick.

Leaving the Lone Star State

DEAR ANNIE: I just graduated from high school in Texas and will be heading to an Ivy League university in a couple of weeks. I graduated as one of the top students in my class. I am also pretty popular. I was captain of the cheerleading team and dated the starting quarterback.

Most of my friends are quintessentially Texan. They play football, cheer, talk about football, hunt, watch football, attend debutante balls and coach football. We are straight out of "Friday Night Lights." I absolutely love Texas. However, I also love the fact that I am getting out of this town.

I love that I will be surrounded by people who are as interested in their schoolwork as I am. I cannot wait to meet my roommate. I am so excited to live on the East Coast. But

I'm also nervous about changing too much at school—losing what makes me Texan.

I want to maintain my Texan roots but explore the world and learn from other cultures. How do I balance embracing new things while staying true to my roots?

—*Prom Queen*

DEAR PROM QUEEN: Something tells me you couldn't shake your Lone Star ways even if you wanted to. (And why would you?) Whatever the stereotypes of Ivy Leagues may be, I guarantee you won't be washed away in a sea of argyle or come home during fall break talking like a Kennedy. The key is never to be embarrassed about who you are—while also being open to learning new things and, yes, maybe even changing a little. In the end, you can take the girl out of Texas, but heaven help the fool who tries to take the Texas out of the girl.

Cheating Among Friends

DEAR ANNIE: My friend "Mary" was dating "Lance." Behind her back, our mutual friend "Sarah" started a physical relationship with Lance while he was still in a relationship with Mary. Mary did not know about this. I was often in the company of the three of them and was uncomfortable watching Lance and Sarah making goo-goo eyes at each other every time Mary turned her back.

Now Mary and Lance have broken up, and Lance has another girlfriend. He is still hooking up with Sarah, behind the other girlfriend's back. Sarah wants to make a go of it with Lance. He has told her that he'll leave the other girlfriend for her. Oy vey!

Here's my question: I am trying to persuade Sarah to tell Mary what's up and ask Mary whether she is OK with her dating Lance. Otherwise, she'll find out through the grapevine. Sarah keeps saying she will talk to Mary, but she hasn't yet. I feel as if I'm in the middle of this ugly, cheating relationship. Mary would be so hurt and angry with me if she found out that Lance had been cheating on her and I knew about it. Or if she didn't find out about the cheating and she just heard about Lance's "new" relationship with Sarah, she'd be hurt I knew about it and said nothing. Do I have any responsibility as a friend here, to either Mary or Sarah?

—*Head Spinning in North Carolina*

DEAR SPINNING: Your head might be spinning, but I guarantee it's still on straighter than Sarah's and Lance's. Those two need to wise up and calm down, Lance in particular. He's spun you and these three women into a very tangled web.

Normally, I tell people not to get in the middle of friends' relationship problems. But I think this situation is a little different, and Mary deserves to hear the truth in a respectful way. It's crummy news no matter what, but it would be better delivered from a close friend than from the gossip mill.

Please advise Mary that she is the luckiest one, whether she realizes it yet or not.

Person Who Needs People

DEAR ANNIE: I am in my mid-60s. I live in a small town, where I know lots of people but have only one friend I can count on. Another really good friend had to move out of state for her job. And another friend, along with her husband, I have known for 35 years, but I get absolutely nothing in return. We only get together if I reach out to her. I'd like to cut her off, but I have no one to take her place.

My extended family members are not too far away, but they are too busy to make a phone call or send an email. I'm friendly with my husband's family members, who all live close by, but they never call or make any effort to keep us informed of family news. My husband has never helped in that regard because he doesn't keep in touch with them, either. He also makes no effort to get together with friends. I have a happy marriage but need more than my husband to keep me company. I need more than one friend, as well.

Having no friends is a problem I have had my whole life. My family of origin was rather dysfunctional, with a brother who was troubled and made it difficult for all of us. My parents were preoccupied with him and expected the rest of us kids to take care of ourselves, and because there were no other kids in the neighborhood to befriend, I feel that I was unprepared to make friends. Looking back now, I could have been a better friend to people as I became an adult but didn't really get it at the time and was very frivolous with friendships. I get along fairly well socially now, but there is no one I can call and say, "Hey, let's do something." I also worry about what would happen if my husband or I got sick, which I'm seeing more with people in our age group. Whom would I call for support?

Facebook makes me sad because it appears that others my

age are still enjoying a very active social life. Has our culture created an atmosphere in which no one cares, or is it just me?

—*Nobody Calls*

DEAR NOBODY CALLS: First off, there aren't any people who are having as good a time as they seem to be on Facebook. If looking at those posts is bringing you down, log off for a while. Second, the best way to get somebody to call is to call her first. I know; you have tried reaching out to some people. But keep trying.

Check out Meetup, a website designed to bring people together in real life over common interests. There's a group for everyone—amateur quantum physicists, alcohol-free adventurers, beer-drinking book-clubbers, puzzle enthusiasts, bridge players; I could go on all day. The point is that you need to get out and try new things. Friends are yours for the making.

Not Gonna Return the Honor

DEAR ANNIE: I was at a dinner party with my girlfriends last week, and we got on the subject of weddings. Someone we know had posted wedding photos on Facebook, and it got us talking about all the details—dress, location, etc. When the wedding party was mentioned, my friend "Jessica" said, "Well, of course, I'll let you girls all pick your dresses when I get married." I looked around and thought, "Me? I would be one of her bridesmaids?" I was pretty stunned. Jessica and I have known each other for years, but we only just started getting to know each other one-on-one a few months ago. She's a lovely girl, and I am glad we are better friends now, but truthfully, I'd feel a little out of place in her wedding party. I mean, her birthday passed in November, and I didn't even have the day memorized. It came and went, and I had no idea. (Whoops.) More importantly, I know I won't ask her to be a bridesmaid at my wedding. I'm dreading that situation. Any thoughts on this?

—Not Always a Bridesmaid

DEAR NAAB: Hold your high heels. From your letter, it doesn't sound as if Jessica is even engaged yet. No need to start sweating her wedding plans. Whenever that time actually comes, the two of you may be much closer and you'll be happy to play an important role in her special day.

And don't worry; you don't have to make someone a bridesmaid purely because you were one of hers. There are so many other factors—the size of your wedding party, whether you have sisters, sisters-in-law or longtime childhood friends to include, etc. A true friend wouldn't hold it against you.

Designated Driver

DEAR ANNIE: I have been friends with a group of women since our high-school days. Since then, some of us have moved out of town, but once a year, we all get together. My problem is that my friends are all heavy drinkers. Because I am the only one who doesn't enjoy drinking, I have always been the designated driver. I didn't like that role in my teens and 20s, but I really resent it now that we're in our 60s.

After dinner, my friends insist on going to pubs to continue their "partying" until the wee hours. As the alcohol flows, my friends become drunk and repetitive and are, frankly, terrible company.

This year, I would like to break with tradition and head home after dinner, but I don't know how to do it without their being furious with me. If I were to leave them after dinner and they were to stay out drinking, they would be angry at having to take costly taxis they can't afford. On the other hand, if they were to leave with me after dinner, they would be livid at my cutting their evening short and being "the party pooper." Because of their peer pressure, I now dread our annual get-togethers. Any advice?

—Designated

DEAR DESIGNATED: If these women grow furious with you for wanting to go home after dinner, they're not friends; they're bullies. It sounds as if you're an obliging, sweet person, and this sweetness has spoiled these women over the years, to the point that they feel entitled to your charity. You shouldn't be punished for not being a lush. And if they can't afford to take taxis, then they shouldn't be spending money on drinks in the first place.

In advance of your next get-together, let them know you won't be the designated driver this year, that you plan on calling it an early night and they should arrange for a cab or use another ride-hailing service. Let them throw their hissy fits; they'll get over it. If they want to keep you as a friend, then they should treat you less like a chauffeur.

I've Gotta Take That

DEAR ANNIE: I have an old and close friend I've known for 50 years. We live far apart, and the only way to talk is by telephone.

Over the past several years, my friend has started to suddenly interrupt our calls when there is a click on the line signaling another call. He will announce midsentence that he has another call coming in that he has to take and then abruptly hang up. He interrupts himself this way as often as he does me. It happens virtually every time we talk, no matter what time it is.

I thought a solution to this might be to ask him to call me when it is convenient for him. That has not stopped this rudeness; he does this even when he has placed the call.

I am at my wits' end and cannot think of a solution short of writing off the friendship. This behavior is very much outside his normal character, which makes it all the more frustrating.

Any ideas on tactfully dealing with this problem?

—I Wasn't Finished

DEAR I WASN'T FINISHED: Don't write off the friendship before you've told your friend how you feel. You should at least let him know these abrupt goodbyes bother you and give him the chance to say his piece. This is a hunch, but is it possible you've not taken verbal cues—such as "Well, it's getting late" or "I should let you go"—that he'd like to end the call? He may be using call waiting as a quick way out.

128

After all, with 50 years' worth of stories, I'm sure you two could talk for hours.

Friends in a Big City

DEAR ANNIE: I moved to New York City for work just over two years ago. Though I grew up in a smaller town in the Midwest and stayed close to home for college, I really love the pace of the city, and I'm starting to feel that I have my place here.

About a month after moving, I was introduced to my now boyfriend, "Josh." We instantly hit it off and have a great, loving relationship. He is from New York originally and has a huge community nearby. Given all his family, co-workers and friends—childhood to college—there's a vast network of people whom I now feel connected with.

NYC can be a difficult place to make friends, and Josh opened up a lot of doors for meeting new people. Yet I still feel as if I'm "Josh's girlfriend" to most of them rather than my own person. True, we mainly see each other when Josh is around, but I'd like to move past that.

Josh's work is sending him to London for three months, and I don't want these friendships to disappear during that time, too. As a fully grown woman, I feel embarrassed to ask, but, Annie, how do I make friends?

—*Big Apple Blues*

DEAR BLUES: No need to feel embarrassed. In many ways,

socializing becomes more challenging once we're "fully grown," as our lives fall into the routine of work, sleep, repeat. It's hard to make friends in the rat race.

But as you've recognized, your current network is an invaluable starting point. Try spending some time, sans Josh, with a few of his friends you feel you have the most in common with.

They in turn can introduce you to other friends and groups, until you've branched out into your own space.

And get active in your community. I would also recommend joining a site such as Meetup, which connects people with similar hobbies and goals—for example, running a marathon, writing a book, learning a new language or learning to cook. Visit https://www.meetup.com for more information.

Friend's Gifts Are Duds

DEAR ANNIE: Christmas has just passed, and once again, I find myself hurt and insulted by my best friend's gift.

I always take such care and pride in choosing just the perfect gift for everyone on my list. I refuse to give a gift card or money, as I feel it's like saying I didn't feel like bothering to shop for that person or don't know the person well enough to know what he or she would like. To me, gifting is a loving gesture, and even if someone chooses something for me that is not perfect, I get pleasure knowing that the person thought of me when choosing the item.

But every year, when I open my best friend's gift, I am disappointed. We've been best friends for 30 years. This year was the worst. It was as if she went through her drawers and gave me everything she didn't want. She gave me foot lotion, a DVD I will never watch, a shirt and a bottle of wine. The foot lotion was in a box that was all tattered and worn. The shirt was her size, not mine, and it smelled like old perfume. The wine was sweet red, and she knows I drink only dry. To top it all off, it was all thrown in a ragged gift bag that said "Happy Birthday"!

I was so hurt. I spent days looking for the perfect gift for her, and I spent a lot of money. I also gave her a huge container of homemade Christmas cookies and candy that she loves.

I have never been one who cares much about what I get; I get my pleasure from giving and knowing I made someone happy. But I just cannot help but be hurt. I haven't spoken to her since Christmas, and she has been texting me, asking whether I liked the gifts. Am I being overly sensitive or selfish by feeling the way I do? Should I confront her about this?

—*Feeling Used in New York*

DEAR FEELING: It sounds as if you're gifted in the art of finding someone just the right present, and that's great. But not everyone is the type. Presents may not be that big of a deal to your friend, or perhaps money's too tight for her to go all out. She did at least try to put something together. If she's a good friend in all other respects, be thankful for that. Keep staring the gift horse in the mouth and it's liable to take a bite out of your friendship.

Help Yourself

DEAR ANNIE: I'm at my wits' end dealing with my friend's glum, woe-is-me attitude. I've known "Max" since we worked together at a restaurant when I was in college. He was in his early 20s and had grown up in the town. He said he regretted not getting a bachelor's degree.

As we became better friends and he saw the projects I was doing for my classes (I was an art major), he became inspired and started making plans to go to community college and then transfer. A year passed; then two. That never happened. (Not a big deal in itself, but I mention it as part of a pattern.)

Six years ago, I graduated and got a job in New York. Max and I have stayed in touch, and he visits about once a year. He's still in the same town, working at a different restaurant. I don't say that judgmentally. I don't think there's anything wrong with it. The problem is that Max does. He's been talking about wanting to change his life for years now, but he takes no steps to do so. I've tried every approach I can think of. I did the supportive thing at first—building up his self-esteem, encouraging him to try therapy, helping him research schools, offering to help get him a restaurant job in New York, etc.

After a couple of years, I realized he wouldn't act on any of this, so I stopped offering solutions and have just shown tough love. For example, when he complains about how none of his friends calls to hang out, I tell him that he can't expect people to always be thinking of him. But nothing seems to get through to him.

Max never asks about what's up in my life, and when I try to tell him, somehow he finds a way of bringing the conversation back to him. I'm starting to feel used and a little resentful, if you couldn't tell. I care about Max and think he's a good guy. But how can you help someone who doesn't really want to help himself?

—*Eeyore's Friend*

DEAR EEYORE'S FRIEND: You can't. At this point, the kindest thing you can do for Max is to refuse to be his dumping ground any longer. Only after he's got nowhere to unload will he be forced to confront the weight of his problem.

A therapist could most likely help him a great deal, and you can encourage him to seek counseling one more time—but disengage and take space after that. Your friendship with Max can only be healthy after he's purged that toxic mindset.

Friend's Fiancé Treats Her Poorly

DEAR ANNIE: I am 20 years old and have been best friends with this girl since we were 5. She's practically my sister. She's engaged to a guy she began dating back in high school. Although he is very nice and genuinely cares for her, he does not seem at all mature enough to be married. After a single semester at a local community college, he left to pursue his dream of becoming a musician. He lives with his grandmother and works at Target. He gets extremely upset if anyone so much as suggests returning to school.

A little under two years ago, they broke up for about two months because he had objections whenever she hung out with any males not related to her. Despite his insisting he trusted her, it was clear he didn't. One night after they had gotten back together, my friend called me sobbing, heartbroken, because he had been jealous and said hurtful things again.

I'm worried that my friend is being naive. She has said she would marry him tomorrow if she could, although she plans on waiting till she is out of school. She has asked me to be a bridesmaid. I can tell that she's trying to make me like the guy better.

I know it is not my place to tell my friend what she should do with her life. I do believe that they love each other, and I want her to be happy, which he seems to make her. But I still fear that she's making a mistake. Is there any way for me to express my concerns without destroying this cherished relationship?

—Looking Out

DEAR LOOKING OUT: It's heartbreaking to see friends treated poorly by significant others. All we ever want to do is to jump in, pull them out of the situation and make sure they never go back. If only it were that easy. You're wise to understand it's not.

As you know, your friend really wants you to like this guy, so the more she senses your disapproval the less she'll open up to you about the reality of the relationship. The best thing you can do is to continue being there for her, ready to listen whenever she's ready to talk, willing to give honest input if and when she asks for it. She's lucky to have you.

Questionable Relationships

DEAR ANNIE: A friend whom I have known for 40-plus years got married for the second time in his life five years ago. At the wedding, some of the bride's relatives told the minister, "These two should not be married." Two years ago, he filed for divorce. In the settlement, he wanted nothing from her. (The house was totally in her name, as was the $15,000 car he bought for her.) After he moved out, he began seeing a psychiatrist, during which time he became very reclusive.

As it stands now, they are once again dating each other. I have no respect for either at this point. By the way, she would never consent to any counseling during their marriage. So why does he seemingly want to go back to her, and why hasn't she asked him, "You didn't want me then, so why should I want to see you again now?"

—*Stumped*

DEAR STUMPED: The question that has me stumped is, What's it to you? This is their relationship, for better or worse. Quit rubbernecking. Keep your eyes on the road. If we all gave as much thought to our own mistakes as we do to everyone else's, perhaps we'd make fewer of them.

Ignored for Others

DEAR ANNIE: I have shared a very close relationship with "Sue" for over 50 years. We worked together as young adults and have remained dear friends throughout the years. We work very closely at our church, as well.

I know I have annoying habits and am thankful for my friends who love me anyway. When it is just the two of us, everything is great with Sue and me. My annoyance with her is that when she is in a conversation with another person (usually before or after church) and I approach and wait (or try to) until they are finished, she does not glance at me or acknowledge my presence at all. I usually just walk away.

When she and I are having a conversation in a similar situation, she'll often stop me when I'm in the middle of saying something so she can speak with every person who passes by. Then I end up walking away because it is so distracting that I honestly can't remember what I was saying.

I recognize this as passive-aggressive behavior, but it puzzles me that she feels the need to control me or shut me down. She is the kindest, most Christian person I know, and I don't know whether she even realizes what she is doing. I don't know why I am writing, because after all of these years, nothing will change. I can't analyze my impact or my aura or how I affect other people. If I could, perhaps I would know how to avoid being blown off as unimportant or insignificant, which is how these situations make me feel.

Perhaps we are both strong personalities and this is her way of being in control. Do you have a suggestion, other than avoiding conversations when others are present?

—Mary

DEAR MARY: For all the talk of conversation here, it sounds as if you've yet to tell Sue how you feel. It's time to change that. I really doubt that she's consciously doing this to try to control you, so give her the benefit of the doubt when raising the topic. Use "I" statements—e.g., "I'm sure you don't mean to do this, but when we're in the middle of talking and you stop to speak with passers-by, I feel ignored"—as opposed to "you" statements, e.g., "You ignore me." True friends appreciate when a friend cares enough to be honest.

Mean Friend

DEAR ANNIE: I have a wonderful group of friends. We all met working together at a restaurant about seven years ago, just out of college. We've really grown up with one another. Two of them are a couple, "Ryan" and "Christine." I love both of them to death, but in all honesty, Christine behaves ridiculously sometimes and is just not nice.

A perfect example: We recently rented a beach house for the weekend, in part to celebrate Christine's birthday. On our first night, we had a barbecue. As we were eating, Ryan reached over and forked a couple of pieces of chicken. Christine scoffed and said, "Are you kidding? It's my birthday, and you're going to take food off my plate without asking?!" Seriously? We were all embarrassed for Ryan and just blown away at how stupid the situation had become.

Now, we're all used to these Christine-isms. She means well. As friends, we're all able to just not pay attention to those moments or confront her if she's downright mean. But we know they have been talking about getting engaged. We see how Ryan looks tired these days. He is truly in love with her, but it seems as if he's exhausted from the relationship. My question is: Should one of us say something to him about it?

—Holding Our Breath

DEAR HOLDING: Keep holding your breath, because you'd probably be better off passing out than getting in the middle of relationship problems. Your heart is in the right place, and it's great Ryan and Christine have friends who care about their well-being. This kind of support will help them have a successful marriage if and when they decide to take that step.

Whoever is closest with Ryan can open up a general, judgment-free dialogue (e.g., "So, how is everything going with you and Christine?") so he feels comfortable talking about any concerns. Likewise, Christine's closest friends might encourage her to work on her temper. But stop short of telling either of them what to do in the relationship, lest you end up taking the heat.

'Omg im so angry'

DEAR ANNIE: My friend "Brianna" and I recently got into a fight via text messaging. She was trying to plan a surprise girls trip for our friend's 30th birthday. She was texting a couple of other friends and me suggestions of places we might go, with links to vacation rentals. The places she was suggesting were out of my price range, though, and I politely said so. We went back and forth on this point for a bit, and then she said, "Well, are you sure you should even go on this trip if it's just not in your budget?"

I couldn't believe she'd be so rude as to say something like that in front of our other friends (digitally, at least). At that point, I just went off and told her she was being selfish. Things devolved from there, and eventually the text conversation ended for the night.

The next day, I felt anxious and regretted the fight. I still wanted to go on this trip, and for the sake of smoothing things over, I sent her a private message apologizing. I expected she would apologize as soon as I did. But to my amazement, all she said was, "It's OK."

"It's OK"? As if I had been in the wrong!

Everyone ended up settling on a local place to celebrate our friend's birthday, and it turns out I can afford to go—but now I'm so angry with Brianna that I don't even want to. Who was wrong, Annie?

—*Sorry Not Sorry*

DEAR SORRY NOT SORRY: You're both wrong for not picking up the phone and calling the second things got tense. Text fights are for people who don't want to find solutions.

But your false apology takes you down another peg. "Sorry" is like "I love you"; you should never say it just to hear it back. It's emotionally manipulative. It's also prone to backfiring. Just look at your predicament. You've painted yourself into a corner, one you can't get out of without looking like a fool and making an even bigger mess. I say swallow your pride on this one and digest the lesson.

Shocking Kiss

DEAR ANNIE: My husband and I went out with another couple for New Year's Eve, "Bob" and "Sheryl." Bob is a longtime friend and has been seeing Sheryl for the past year. Here's the issue: After the clock struck midnight and everyone was sharing well-wishes and kisses and hugs, Sheryl decided to put her tongue down my husband's throat and plant an extensive kiss on him, all while Bob and I were right there! Granted, there definitely was alcohol involved, but I don't lose my faculties and forget whom I came with when I drink.

I, in turn, stated that she had crossed the line, gathered our things and left. She attempted to say she was sorry upon our departure; however, I just couldn't stay the rest of the evening knowing she did this to our friendship. My husband had no idea what was happening and felt he didn't encourage this behavior. He had been seated by me the entire evening.

So now none of us has spoken about it and things are just awkward when we run into them in public. I'm so sad that our friendship with Bob can be no more, because he remains with Sheryl. How should we move past this transgression? Or is it just avoidance from here on out?

—Betrayed in PA

DEAR BETRAYED: Wait it out and let this situation resolve itself. Be polite when you run into Bob and Sheryl, and don't go around bad-mouthing her. I have a hunch that if Sheryl is kissing married men in front of Bob, by next New Year's Eve she'll be out of the picture.

Sick of the Negativity

DEAR ANNIE: I'm writing to you regarding one of my best friends, "Melanie." Melanie and I are both in our late 20s. We met in college and bonded over our senses of humor and our preference for staying in and watching a movie over going out to frat parties. She's been there for me during some hard times. She's one person I can rely on to always answer my calls and be there for me, and I appreciate her.

But she seems unable or unwilling to get out of the rut she's been in for the past few years, and it's become increasingly frustrating to listen to her complaining about the same things every day. She took a retail job out of college, just to make ends meet until she could find something in her field. Five years later and she's still there, and in the meantime, I've had to hear about it pretty much every day.

I've tried to help her look for jobs and sent her lots of links to job postings, but I'm pretty sure she hasn't actually applied to any of them. She always has a list of reasons—e.g., "I'm not really qualified for that," "I don't have time to apply for jobs," "I need to update my resume." She tends to play the victim in a lot of areas of her life.

And that's part of why I'm scared to confront her. I want to tell her that she's been talking about these same problems for years and it's time to change, but I know she'd be offended.

Lately, I find myself screening her phone calls because when I get home from a long day of work, I just don't want to hear the negativity. I feel bad for avoiding her. I want to be a good friend. What should I do?

—Emotionally Exhausted

DEAR EMOTIONALLY: It's frustrating to watch a friend languishing in a rut that she could easily climb out of. But if you tried to yank her out of it, she'd only pull you down into the wallowing hole with her, and that would be a toxic place to be. So keep a healthy distance between you and that aspect of her, not just for your sake but also for hers; by listening to her venting about the same problems every day, you're actually enabling her not to change.

Draw the line. Tell her your New Year's resolution is to not dwell on negatives. Whenever she starts up the "woe is me" routine, tell her that you're happy to discuss solutions but if she just wants to talk about the same problems again, you're not able to listen. Eventually—let's hope—she'll get out of that rut all on her own. That will give her the self-confidence to keep the momentum going.

Unofficial Third Roommate

DEAR ANNIE: Recently, I moved into an apartment with my

friend "Grace." Since we moved in, Grace's boyfriend, "Jesse," has been spending a lot of time at our place. He stores his groceries in our refrigerator, and they often shower in our (shared) bathroom together while I'm home.

Last week, he brought a suitcase over, and he has spent every night here since. I think Jesse's a nice guy, but I'm uncomfortable having him as our pseudo third roommate (who doesn't even pay rent). It feels like a violation of my personal space. I don't want my friendship with Grace to be strained. What is the best way to handle this?

—Frustrated Friend

DEAR FRUSTRATED FRIEND: Meet with Grace for an open conversation about expectations and boundaries. Together you can come up with a list of house rules, not just regarding how many nights a week boyfriends are allowed to stay but also regarding cleaning, parties, quiet hours, etc. You'll both need to make compromises—but be honest with yourselves and each other about what you're willing to accept. Agreeing to a rule that you secretly think is unfair now would only lead to resentment down the road, which would defeat the whole purpose of the document in the first place. And yes, it should be a document—something written down and signed by you both.

This might sound too rigid or formal for friends. But trust me; if you want your friendship to survive your lease, you're going to need ground rules.

Stop With the Subtweeting

DEAR ANNIE: My best friend and I have been friends for over 15 years now, and we get along very well and definitely know each other better than anyone else. However, we are very different people. I guess you could say that I am a lot simpler than she is. I don't really beat around the bush, whereas she is passive-aggressive; and I am on the quiet side, while she likes to be heard.

She has been complaining to me a lot about the drama she has in her life, and I don't mind. I am always there for her, whether it's to give my straightforward opinion or just to listen to her rambling on the phone in the middle of the night. When we are communicating openly, it's great.

But, Annie, the issue is that she has taken things to another level, and I have no control over it. She is very active on Twitter, and I don't have an account, much less an understanding of the social media platform.

A few close mutual friends have been telling me that she has been passive-aggressively tweeting about me in a negative way—and it's very obvious that it's about me. I don't understand. I am always there for her, and I am open and honest when we communicate. But when I don't understand what I've done wrong, it's hard to grasp any understanding of what to fix.

I would like to ask her what her deal is, but I don't know how to do so because I'm obviously pretty miffed that she is being so publicly passive-aggressive and I am offended. But I also don't want her to get upset with our other friends, because it will be obvious that they shared the information with me. I am in a bit of a strange pickle here and would love your input. I don't want there to be any unspoken issues between my best friend and me, but I don't know how to deal with this rude and immature behavior.

—*Anti-Social Media*

DEAR ANTI-SOCIAL: Rude and immature is right. Passive-aggressive behavior has always been exasperating. Social media have taken it to a new level.

The best approach in dealing with such people is to refuse to play their game. Be positive but direct. Tell her that you saw her Twitter page (no need to mention that your mutual friends told you) and were concerned by the tweets. Don't let her wriggle out of it. Try to get her to admit that she's upset with you, thus denying her the ability to keep silently sulking. At the end of the day, she should respect you for holding her accountable. Friends don't let friends get away with passive-aggressive behavior.

Odd Woman Out

DEAR ANNIE: I was recently placed in a troubling situation that I think really exemplifies the struggles of practicing what you preach. I am part of a large group of friends that formed a giant group-text chain that we all communicate in; it's a nice and easy way to stay in touch while we're in different places, and having the comfort of a dozen other girls be just the push of a few keys away is great. Obviously, some in the group are closer than others, but it's nice for all of us to be able to feel as if we belong to something.

145

One of the girls, "Priscilla," is much more on the outside than the others. Recently, a few of us were together, and one of the girls, "Gabby," decided she was going to remove this "odd woman out" from the phone group. I was uncomfortable with the situation, but instead of arguing, I turned my head and kept my mouth shut, wanting to claim no part in it.

Priscilla reached out to all of us the next day, asking whether she had been removed. Gabby told her that we had gotten rid of the conversation altogether.

Annie, Priscilla must know that she was removed. I have been bullied before and have always been very vocal about standing up for what is right, and now I realize that I had the opportunity to stop this from happening but I kept my mouth shut. As a result of this mess, the group chat actually did come to an end, most likely out of everyone else's guilt. The hard part is that these people are all my friends. I want to reach out to Priscilla, but I know she will ask me what the truth is, and I can't rat out another friend. I don't want to have to pick between people I care about or cause problems among friends. I'm disappointed in myself, but more importantly, I want to make it right. What do you think the right thing is to do here?

—Fraidy-Cat Friend

DEAR FRAIDY-CAT: Though the technology is new, the dilemma is timeless. Being part of a group feels great—but that feeling so often relies on keeping others out. Gabby is being shortsighted and selfish. And to be a true friend to her, you ought to tell her as much. We all need friends to yank us back down to earth occasionally. Encourage her to apologize to Priscilla. If she refuses or makes excuses, then it's time to step in and talk to Priscilla yourself, empathize and reconsider your friendship with Gabby.

Too Busy to Be a Friend

DEAR ANNIE: I have Type 2 diabetes, and I went through a near-death experience this summer—with kidney failure, congestive heart failure and other problems. I had to have surgery. While I recovered in the hospital, my son brought me my laptop. I posted my story on Facebook.

While my other friends were offering messages of sympathy over my illness, my friend "Jill" was posting about an art show she was having. She paid no attention to my post. After a couple of weeks, I texted her husband, "Jack," and asked whether Jill had seen my post. I repeated my whole story. He said that Jill was too busy to talk, that she had an upcoming art show and their son was getting married. After another couple of weeks, I texted, "How was the wedding?" I found that the wedding was not for another two weeks. Yet Jill has not said anything about my brush with death.

I still have a tiny amount of fluid in my pericardium, and my left ventricle is still enlarged. What happened in June could recur, and next time, I might not be so lucky. I recently read that when we are handed bad news that is too much for us to handle, our minds settle on lesser problems that we can focus our grief and anger on. This made a lot of sense to me. I cannot wrap my head around dying, so I can be angry with my self-absorbed friends.

But what should I do? Jill was a good friend.

She may have a chip on her shoulder about having flunked grad school while some of us went on to have exciting tech jobs. She found her niche later in life, maybe in her 50s, and has fallen into a habit of dismissing those of us who are retired.

—*Miffed*

DEAR MIFFED: Yes, you're probably focusing so much on Jill because it's easier to be angry at something tangible. You hit that square on the head. Then you went right back to resenting her.

You need to break this cycle of blame and judgment—not for Jill's sake but for your own. When recovering from surgery and battling chronic illness, attitude is everything. Start a gratitude journal, and list 10 things you're grateful for every morning. Spend time with friends and family who make you feel loved.

Jill may come around eventually and apologize for not being there. She may not. Your mood can't depend on it. Forgive her in your heart and free yourself to experience more joy. I wish you good health.

Discussing Relationship Problems

DEAR ANNIE: My boyfriend, "Hector," and I have been dating for four years. Like any couple, we've had our ups and downs. We used to argue a lot about things that were, in retrospect, petty and inconsequential. The beginning of last year was especially bad. We had each hit a wall professionally. We were always frustrated and stressed out, and though it was for reasons that had nothing to do with each other, it inevitably affected the way we treated each other.

During this rocky time, I talked to my good friend "Michelle" a lot about the problems Hector and I were having. I'm not one to brag about my relationship when things are going well, so this was the first Michelle was really hearing details about my relationship, and they were all bad. As good friends do, Michelle immediately took my side in the fight (even when I was wrong) and built me up and told me I deserved to be treated better.

Fast-forward a year. Hector and I have hugely improved our communication skills and are happier than ever. We talk about marriage regularly. I really think he's the one.

The problem now is that Michelle still hates him. OK, maybe "hate" is too strong a word, but she's definitely not a fan. I tried talking to her about it. I told her that I know she got a bad impression of Hector from things I said but that we have worked on our communication and are doing much better. She said something like "that's great," but I knew she didn't mean it.

I feel that I should never have opened up to Michelle about the problems we were having. How can you talk to friends about your relationship problems without their judging your relationship?

—*Foot in Mouth*

DEAR FOOT IN MOUTH: You can't. That's why the only person with whom you should be discussing your relationship problems is the person with whom you're in that relationship. It's not just the most respectful option; it's the most constructive, because he or she is the only person who can actually help solve the problem.

Michelle will come around in time, if Hector continues to be a good boyfriend. But take this experience as a lesson for the future and refrain from talking badly about your boyfriend to your friends. I must note that abuse is an important exception to this advice. Readers, if you feel unsafe, please reach out to friends or call The National Domestic Violence Hotline at 800-799-7233.

Back Off, Friends

DEAR ANNIE: I have many close friends from different groups. My time with each of them is very important, and I don't want to be tied down to one friend. My partner has many wonderful friends he enjoys spending time with, too.

Recently, we got acquainted with another couple at my young son's football match. The newfound friendship is moving too fast. They are already talking about doing weekends away together, planning several weekend trips for us all. We've only known them for a few months and been friends for a month.

I'm a pretty easygoing, kind-natured woman; I fit in with all types of crowds. But I don't like to be pushed into things or backed into a corner. I like things to take a slow, natural course, and I never rush the process of becoming close with someone.

I don't believe friendships or relationships work well when they progress quickly. My partner and I were friends for seven years before we started dating! I feel uncomfortable with what's developing. I have this uneasy feeling about the progress of this new friendship. My hunches are normally accurate, and I'm an OK judge of character. Am I being a little childish about this? What should I do?

—Too Fast for Me

DEAR TOO FAST: What's stopping you from pumping the brakes? There's a simple solution here—saying "No, thank you" or "We're busy" to the weekend-getaway invitations. As you don't seem to have entertained that option, I'm guessing you're the type of person who has a hard time saying no.

I'd encourage you to do some self-reflection regarding why that is. Perhaps you value being seen as easygoing more than you value your own needs and wants. Work on setting boundaries.

Happy in the Country

DEAR ANNIE: I currently live in a small town in rural Missouri. I grew up here, and my husband grew up here, and we plan on raising our own family here, as well. The only time I left was for college. I moved to St. Louis for four years and enjoyed the new adventures of big-city life, but I moved back home right after graduation. One of my best college girlfriends, "Jessica," who's also from here, recently moved back for family reasons after having stayed in the city for another five years.

Annie, my issue is that Jessica is always complaining to me about how boring our hometown is and how she can't wait to leave, and she draws out old college experiences to make me agree with her.

I've tried telling her that though I did love being in a big city, I'm really a small-town person. However, she refuses to listen and keeps pressuring me to move back to St. Louis with her. Don't I miss the culture? The art? The restaurants? The job opportunities? Well, yes, sometimes. But I'm happy here. And I'm happy Jessica is here, too. When not complaining, she's an incredible friend. How do I keep my friendship without disregarding my town?

—*Country Catie*

DEAR COUNTRY CATIE: It's time to remind your city-loving friend of the value of small-town humility. Be very clear with Jessica that though you appreciate and understand what she loves about a big city, you and your husband prefer the quiet of the country. Tell her that when she's not complaining, she's an incredible friend.

In the end, she will appreciate your honesty. And perhaps it will cause her to pause and reflect on her current life, what's making her unhappy and what she could do to change it—as opposed to reminiscing about her glory days in college.

Lunches With a Controlled Wife

DEAR ANNIE: I am concerned about one of my friends, "Amanda." She and I are both middle-aged housewives with only part-time jobs. For the past six months or so, we've been having lunch together once a week.

Amanda comes from a much more repressed background than I do. She was raised to believe that wives should be submissive to their husbands, etc.

Our weekly lunch is in a restaurant that's located inside a supermarket. I like the food there. Amanda used to say she liked the location because when her husband asked about her day, she could truthfully tell him she had only gone to the grocery. She said it would take time for her to let him know about having a new friend.

Amanda has complained about her controlling husband. She told me he checks her phone and email all the time. However, she has such an upbeat, happy disposition, I thought she was exaggerating. About a month ago, she told me that since she's gotten to know me, she's had the courage to speak up to her husband about some things for the very first time, and it has led to some positive changes in their marriage.

The next week, Amanda's husband just showed up with her at our lunch. I welcomed meeting him because I knew he could see that I'm a straight woman who poses no threat.

Since then, however, he has come with her every week. He owns his own business, so he must have rearranged his whole schedule to lunch with us! He sits with us but doesn't say much. He mostly plays with his phone. Of course, my conversation with Amanda is quite different with him sitting there. This whole thing seems weird to me. I'm afraid that if I were to say much, our lunches would end altogether. Do you have any suggestions?

—Silenced in the Supermarket

DEAR SILENCED: Though you might be limited in what you can say to Amanda, your mere presence speaks volumes. It tells her she's not alone—that someone cares. To someone in an abusive relationship, that's an invaluable message. And that's why the best thing you can do for Amanda right now is to continue attending these lunches and pretending her husband's presence is welcome. Any perceived rejection of him would be used to separate you from her.

Call The National Domestic Violence Hotline (800-799-7233) for more guidance.

Its Name Is Gossip

DEAR ANNIE: I need advice on how to deal with my husband's friend. This person is a gossip who delves into the details of other people's personal lives. He entertains groups with these unflattering stories and makes himself important by offering his analyses, judging their life choices, misdeeds and daily activities.

Family, friends and anyone in the public eye are subject to his scrutiny. He can be quite charming while he's being friendly with you during his "information gathering" stage, but he has hurt many people and tarnished their reputations. He is a bully and a poor role model.

He claims to be religious and caring, but I find his behavior intrusive and offensive. He questions my husband about our family activities on a daily basis. I have told my husband and this person that this is unacceptable. I try hard to avoid him. Why are some people such gossip-mongers?

—*Fed Up by This Octopus*

DEAR FED UP: You're smart to stay out of his toxic tentacles' reach. I'm surprised this man still has friends at all. If someone gossips about anyone not in the room, you know whom he'll be talking about just as soon as you're out the door. Let's hope your husband will put that together in time and cut ties with this man.

Below is a poem called "Nobody's Friend" (author unknown), which several readers have shared with me:

> *My name is Gossip.*
> *I have no respect for justice.*
> *I maim without killing.*
> *I break hearts and ruin lives.*
> *I am cunning and malicious and gather strength with age.*
> *The more I am quoted the more I am believed.*
> *I flourish at every level of society.*
> *My victims are helpless.*
> *They cannot protect themselves against me because I have no name and no face.*
> *To track me down is impossible.*
> *The harder you try, the more elusive I become.*
> *I am nobody's friend.*
> *Once I tarnish a reputation, it is never the same.*
> *I topple governments and ruin marriages.*

I ruin careers and cause sleepless nights, heartache and indigestion.

I spawn suspicion and generate grief.

I make innocent people cry in their pillows.

Even my name hisses.

I am called Gossip.

◆

HOW DO I KNOW IF I'M MOVING THERE FOR HIM OR MOVING THERE FOR ME?

Love

Mr. Perfect

DEAR ANNIE: I feel like a cliché. I feel so stupid. It wasn't supposed to be like this. I'm 34. I graduated from one Ivy League university and got a master's from a different one. I don't look like Scarlett Johansson, but I'm above average in the looks department. I get my hair highlighted. I work out. I dress well. Yet I'm single.

I told myself it wouldn't bother me. I leaned in to my career. I went on dates, but no guy ever felt like the one. I had a few casual relationships but didn't do the whole "he's OK for right now" thing. If I wasn't super into him, I let him go. And I really haven't met a guy I've been super into.

I never did the online dating thing. I just wasn't focused on it. I have a friend who is obsessed with it. She downloads every app and talks about it nonstop. She talks about dating the way men talk about fantasy football.

I was supposed to have it all—to be happily married with children. I don't want to leave my career, but I am 34 and want a family. I don't want to settle for some schlub, either.

—*Cliché Cathy*

DEAR CLICHÉ: You're not waiting for Mr. Right; you're waiting for Mr. Perfect. There's no such thing. Why haven't you been into the guys you've seen in the past? What's been missing? There's a difference between having some basic criteria (e.g., "respectful," "employed," "not Norman Bates") and having an elaborate, Westminster Dog Show-style rubric. Be more open.

And please, in no way, shape or form do you have to leave your career for a husband or family. Plenty of women with successful careers are wives and mothers, too—including me.

'Just Kidding' 35 Years Later

DEAR ANNIE: My husband and I have been married for more than 40 years. During the first five years of our marriage, he confessed to several instances of infidelity. He begged for forgiveness. I forgave him.

Well, recently, I found out he was lying and never actually had slept with other women. He told me that he had been questioning my loyalty and made up situations to see whether I loved him enough to forgive him and that I had passed the test. Well, yes, I forgave him each time because I loved him, but my feelings about him did change a little from the hurt of the supposed infidelity. I went through hell internally back then, but I didn't let him know.

I don't understand what would make someone do that. He has been an excellent husband for the past 35 years, but I could have had a much better marriage had he not lied the first five years. I can't stop thinking of how things could have been and what the real truth is. What would you suggest I do?

—*Happy or Sad*

DEAR HAPPY OR SAD: If he truly was making up these lies about cheating as some kind of test of your loyalty, that's pretty twisted. If he did cheat but now has decided to rewrite history and pretend he wasn't an adulterer, that's pretty twisted, too. Which is true? At this point, the more important question is why he would jerk you around like this at all. Such emotional abuse is unacceptable.

Tell your husband that if you're to ever free yourselves from the tangled web he's woven, it will be through marriage counseling. If he refuses, I encourage you to attend counseling on your own.

An Ex Wants More

DEAR ANNIE: Three years ago, my former high school sweetheart and I had a one-night stand. We both live in different states, but I was visiting my family.

Although we didn't have intercourse, he seems to dwell on this night.

For example, when he knew that I was planning a visit the following year, he booked a hotel room. I never encouraged him to do that or indicated that we'd get together again. In my opinion, he was being presumptuous. He saw it as being hopeful.

I have been in a long-term relationship and felt guilty about the one-night stand. I love the man deeply. The ex wished him dead. He said he was joking. I say that many a truth is spoken in jest.

I communicate with him occasionally, but that's only because I have a sibling who was in a tumultuous relationship and the ex would tell me about any drama associated with that. But in texts and phone conversations, he talks suggestively, inappropriately and rude, getting too intimate. He's declared, "I'll never give up" and "It'll never be over." I know that he's not involved with anyone. My question: Is this obsessive behavior?

—*Confused*

DEAR CONFUSED: If you really want this man to stop holding a candle for you, all you have to do is blow it out. I'm not convinced you do. The situation with your sibling is no excuse to stay in touch, and the fact that you've continued talking to him on such dubious grounds suggests you might be getting something out of these exchanges after all— validation, perhaps. That's not healthy.

It's time to shut it down. Tell this man, in no uncertain terms, that you have zero romantic interest in him and you want him to stop contacting you. Block his number. If he starts stalking you or seriously threatening your boyfriend's safety, document everything and take out a restraining order. But I have a feeling this old Romeo won't come calling if he sees that the balcony door is closed, locked and boarded.

Is It Just a Game?

DEAR ANNIE: My wife is borderline addicted to "Words With Friends" (an app game similar to Scrabble), and it's causing me concern, in addition to creating some strife within our marriage. It would be one thing if she were only playing with other female players, but she also has an ongoing game with a former male classmate, which I consider to be a form of online flirting. Would you agree, or am I overreacting?

I still work, and my wife is retired, so when I'm ready for bed because I have to get up early, she is wide-awake and ready for late-night games with friends (one in particular). I have suggested repeatedly that she go to bed when I go, but she says she isn't sleepy and is a late-night person, so she stays up until 1 or 2 a.m. playing "Words With Friends." This continues to cause disharmony in our marriage, and it's something I have a hard time accepting as permissible. Please let me know how you and your readers feel about this issue.

—Concerned Husband

DEAR CONCERNED HUSBAND: Unless she's exchanging flirty messages with this old classmate or spelling out inappropriate words on the board, I wouldn't worry about the fact that she's playing with him. There's nothing wrong with connecting with old friends to play games online. There is, however, something wrong with allowing anything to consume your life—be it alcohol, drugs, work, television or even "Words With Friends."

Ask her whether she's game for a challenge: She uninstalls the app for two weeks; you commit to getting home from work on time and planning a few date nights during that period.

If she's unwilling to give up an app for two weeks for the health of her marriage, then this is a deeper problem that requires the help of a counselor.

An Old Flame

DEAR ANNIE: In December, I went to a holiday house party, and most of the people in the crowd were my old friends from college (class of 1979). I hadn't seen some of these people in 25 years or more. The hostess pulled out her giant photo album, and there they were, several pictures of my favorite ex-girlfriend and me having the time of our lives. I haven't seen or talked to her since 1985.

So my big question is: Would it be kosher to write her a light and lively letter and catch up? We've both been married with kids for close to 30 years. (I looked her up online.)

She's the one who got away from me, but I'm not looking for any do-over; we had our chances. But I would pay big money for a time machine! What do you think?

—*Nostalgic in Boston*

DEAR NOSTALGIC: No matter how many years have passed, to reconnect with this old flame would be playing with fire, and your whole family would be liable to get burned.

If you didn't feel that this woman was the one who got away, I would say sure, you could strike up a friendship. But because you're still wishing for a time machine, I think you'd better keep your distance. I'd also recommend taking off those rose-colored glasses when looking at your past. There was a reason you two broke up. Reminisce about your college days as much as you'd like, but don't try to resurrect them.

Back on the Scene

DEAR ANNIE: I need some guidance. I'm new to the dating scene after my very long-term relationship fell apart earlier this year. I feel like a newbie. What's normal? I haven't dated in almost 10 years. Back when I was on the scene before, people weren't all meeting each other through apps. That whole prospect scares me, so I've been trying to meet guys the old-fashioned way so far.

Anyway, I've been seeing this guy for a little over a month, but we've only gone on four dates. Is that average, or is he not interested? My most recent boyfriend and I lived together for several years, so I'm used to hanging out almost every day. I find myself wanting to text or call this guy throughout the week. I don't want to suffocate him, but if he's not really into me, I'd like to find out so I can move on.

—Anxious

DEAR ANXIOUS: I know it's easier said than done, but for goodness' sake, relax. Going out once a week is normal. Enjoy the slow pace, and focus on yourself. If love is going to kindle between you two, it will need oxygen.

Bye, Bicoastal Love

DEAR ANNIE: I've been on-again, off-again with this guy for five years. We're both musicians. We live on opposite coasts, but between touring and picking up studio gigs, we cross paths or end up in each other's city every couple of months.

We were only "official" for about a year, three years ago. We decided to end things because of the distance. But we couldn't just cut things off completely, so we continued to stay in touch via texts and phone calls—as "friends." The next time he was in town, we met up for a drink, and long story short, we ended up spending the whole weekend together. We've done that routine a few times a year ever since.

It's been confusing. We're both technically single, but I've always felt as if I'm in a relationship. I don't have any interest in dating anyone else, and I thought he felt the same way—until last month.

I was going to be in his city for work. I texted him a couple of weeks prior to let him know I'd be in town, and he said he couldn't wait. Then, as the date got closer, he went radio-silent. He stopped responding to any of my texts and didn't answer my calls. Finally, I sent him a long text telling him how angry and hurt I was. He responded with a text telling me he started seeing someone else recently and doesn't want to mess it up.

I feel betrayed and hurt, but maybe worst of all, I can't help but hold out hope that this is just a fling and he'll want me back when it's over. We've had such a good thing for so long.

I want to tell him I'd even be willing to relocate if he wanted to try to make it work. But I just don't know where he really stands. It feels as if everything he's said and done for the past five years has sent mixed signals. I wish he would just be straight with me. Help.

—Long-Distance Limbo

DEAR LONG-DISTANCE: He gave you an answer loud and clear, but you've been covering your ears. I don't blame you, as it sounds as if he's been leading you on quite a bit over the past five years. But it's time to face the fact that this man is not interested in a serious relationship with you. The truth hurts, but it will set you free. And should this guy come crawling back in a few months, have enough love for yourself to tell him no.

A Flicker of Co-Worker Romance

DEAR ANNIE: I am a 31-year-young man with a question about a woman who is 28. This story started in August of last year with my asking this woman on a date. We work together but were in different departments at the time. She said she doesn't date the people she works with. I didn't buy it, so I kept flirting with her. And she'd flirt back.

This went on until December of that year, when we saw each other in a neighborhood bar. She came up to my friend and me and pulled on the hood of my sweatshirt. Then she started to walk away, but my friend stopped her by standing in front of her. I talked to her like normal. Then I kissed her on the cheek. Then my friend left, and we hugged. I rubbed her back, and she rubbed mine. I kissed her hand. Then she turned away, and I playfully smacked her on the butt. We left at the same time but went our separate ways. The next day, we saw each other at work, and she came over to me and gave me a peck on the cheek.

After that, it all went downhill. I saw her sitting on another guy's lap at work. (He works in a different department than we do.) I took it personal. Here she was, the girl I was attracted to, sitting on this guy's lap.

I felt as if she'd lied to me. I think that maybe she'd forgotten I asked her out, but I have told her I want her to be my girlfriend on several occasions. So I think she knows how I feel about her. After all this, I'm not sure what to think. Any help would be appreciated.

—*Pining*

DEAR PINING: Dating co-workers is great—if your goal is to save time by simultaneously ruining your personal life and your career. I would like to know why you didn't buy it when this woman told you she doesn't date co-workers, because you should have bought it, thrown away the receipt and gotten the message in your head, even if she later sent mixed signals.

Save yourself a lot of strife and look for love outside the workplace. Yes, we all know happily married couples who met across the watercooler. In the right circumstances with mature individuals (and maybe a consultation with HR), it can be done. But this sounds like an astonishingly immature group. Case in point: Unless it's Bring Your Child to Work Day, no one should be sitting on anyone's lap at the office.

New City, New Heart

DEAR ANNIE: My girlfriend, "Lucy," and I started dating three years ago, during our senior year of college. After graduating, we both got jobs in the same city where we had gone to school, and we ended up moving in together to save money. Living together was surprisingly easy, as we're both pretty low-maintenance people. Anyway, Lucy is a good partner. She's always encouraged me to push myself to pursue my passions. She's the reason I ended up applying to a dream job even though it was across the country. I never thought I'd actually end up landing it. But I did.

I moved out here last month. The plan was for me to come out first and get settled in my job; then Lucy would follow a few months later. Things are going really well. The company I'm working for is a perfect fit; there's so much to see and do in the city, and I've already made some friends.

The problem is I'm having second thoughts about Lucy.She's a great person, and I wouldn't even be out here if it weren't for her encouragement. But I just don't find myself feeling the same sparks. I feel terrible writing these words, but I don't really miss her. When I see her name lighting up my phone, I have to force myself to answer it.

She's flying out for a visit soon to see my new place and apply to some restaurant jobs before making the move. I don't know what to do. Should I just wait for her to and see how things go? Or do I need to break it off before then?

—Feeling Guilty

DEAR FEELING GUILTY: If you're feeling guilty now, imagine how you'll feel if she moves there. It's time to end things. Keep it short and sweet. Thank her for the years you've shared, and then tell her you want to break up. Have this talk sooner rather than later. You're not doing her any favors by dating her out of a sense of obligation. She deserves someone whose face lights up when her name lights up his phone. Let her go find him.

Crushing on Friend of 40 Years

DEAR ANNIE: My wife and I divorced in 2007 after 33 years of marriage; after the kids moved out, she realized she didn't love me anymore. I'm writing because I have a crush on a woman with whom I've been friends for 40 years.

Her late husband was a very good friend of mine. My now-ex-wife and I used to socialize with them as couples. He and I hunted and fished and talked about everything in that special way you can when you're on a boat, no one else listening. Our wives did their own things together.

They were married for 25 years, until he passed away in 2013. At his funeral, we said our goodbyes, and she insisted on walking me to my vehicle, which was a block away. We hugged, and she said, "Don't be a stranger. Maybe we could go out to dinner." So I waited six months or so and asked her out to dinner. She accepted, and since 2014 we have been going out twice a month and spending Christmas, New Year's Eve and both our birthdays together. I always pay, except on my birthday; then she insists on buying.

I haven't been in a rush, but lately I find myself attracted more and more. When our evenings are over and I take her home, we exchange a handshake or a peck on the cheek, and I respect her too much to push more of an advance than that.

She is 60, and I am 65. She works full time, and I'm semi-retired. I haven't dated since I was very young. Do I stay the course?

—*Unfamiliar Waters*

DEAR UNFAMILIAR: Stay the course, sailor. The conditions look perfect. You two could offer each other companionship as you glide into your golden years. Birthdays, holidays and biweekly dinners together? You two must be best friends. That is a wonderful foundation for a relationship, and it sounds as if you're already going through many of the motions of dating. Make your intentions known by asking whether she would like to go on a date. One of the upsides of dating at 65 versus 16 is maturity and understanding. If you ask her out and she's not interested, you can stay friends. No awkwardly dodging each other in homeroom.

Dealing With Debilitating Grief

DEAR ANNIE: I am a 69-year-old man who, until now, only read your column periodically. Each time I read your advice to someone, I would say to myself, "Hmm, that's really good advice." I never ever thought that I would need to write to you. Well, now I am eating those words.

In late August, I lost the most important person in my life to inoperable pancreatic cancer. My wife was diagnosed in June 2014, and despite the fact that the cancer spread to three additional organs, she fought back.

This amazing woman refused to let the cancer win. She went on with her life, and even though she received chemo and radiation therapy on a regular basis, as well as numerous medications, she refused to give in.

I drove her to every doctor's appointment and every radiation and chemotherapy appointment, as well as all over the country as we searched for clinical trials. However, after two-plus years, her fragile body could fight no longer, and she died in my arms.

The reason I am writing to you is that I am a total mess. Friends and family are calling me to come to dinner. I don't want to be around people as I grieve; I prefer to be alone all of the time. Our house is just as it was on the day she died because I simply can't part with her things at this time. Yet seeing these things sends me into pain and sobbing sessions that may last for hours. I have completely lost faith in everything, and I don't trust professionals. I have joined several grief support groups, but I do not find solace in them yet.

My wife and I spent 50 years of our lives together. She was my best friend, my soul mate and my only love. Without her, I feel empty and incomplete. Although people keep telling me that things eventually will get better, I have my doubts. I am trying to take care of myself and to do the things I believe she would want me to do if she were still alive. The only thing I really have difficulty doing is sleeping. I would appreciate any advice you can offer.

—*Neil*

DEAR NEIL: I know that nothing I say can reduce the enormity of your loss—that my response may come across as clichéd or maybe even a little hollow—because in the face of such grief, words look ridiculous and small. Still, I must say, with all of my heart, that I am so sorry for your loss.

In these times of deep grief, turn to the memories you and your wife shared. Let them warm you through the night like a blanket. They are eternal. No one can ever take those away from you. Your wife lives on in your heart. Let her strength help you through this.

Be patient with yourself and permit yourself to grieve as long and as deeply as you need. But it sounds as if your wife was an amazing fighter, and she would want you to fight—to be strong, to wring as much joy and happiness out of life as you possibly can, every single glorious day on this earth.

You are blessed to have friends and family who want to lift you up. When you are ready, you will let them. One day, someone close to you will find himself in this same unfathomable situation, and your friendship will be his saving grace. Think how proud your wife would be to see you spread that love.

Heart Left on the East Coast

DEAR ANNIE: I am from Northern California. I went to college back east and worked in New York for three years after school. My wife and I met in Manhattan.

About four months after we started dating, I got into a prestigious law school in Northern California, which made the future of the relationship come to the forefront: Fish or cut bait?

We stayed together. She moved out to this coast and got a master's degree, and we slowly built lives together in California. That was eight years ago.

Our lives are good. We own a nice home. We have a dog and a kid on the way. However, my wife is not happy.

Every few weeks, she gets homesick. Not like slightly melancholy, more like in bed, crying, depressed homesick. She says that she misses her family but also the changing seasons of the East Coast. The monotonous climate that we live in makes her sad.

I am a problem-solver. I've tried to fix the problem (e.g., nice house, trips to the East Coast, flying out family), but I am at the end of my rope. I am open to moving back, but my career is kind of taking off. Both of our careers are, actually. It would be very difficult to press the reset button. I can't keep dealing with her and her emotions. I don't know what else to do.

—Geographically Challenged

DEAR GEOGRAPHICALLY CHALLENGED: Though it might seem that your wife gets depressed because she's homesick, it's equally possible that she's homesick because she's depressed. The debilitating nature of her sadness seems to indicate the latter. I'd encourage her to seek the guidance of a professional therapist to develop habits for a healthy emotional state regardless of her geographical state. After all, wherever you go, there you are.

Deciding Between Two Guys

DEAR ANNIE: I am torn between two guys. I have liked Guy No. 1 for a while. I first saw him across a campus courtyard last fall, and I was smitten. After months of nervously trying to work up the courage to approach him, I finally talked to him at a party a couple of months ago. And to my shock, he ended up liking me, too. We went on a few dates. He cooked me dinner, which was nice. We've had to pause things for the summer because he's traveling, but we plan on seeing each other when he gets back.

Then there's Guy No. 2. He's been my friend for two years. Though I didn't really have romantic feelings for him, there was some small level of attraction. But he never expressed any interest until I started going on dates with Guy No. 1.

The problem with Guy No. 1 is I don't feel quite so passionately about him now that I actually know him. He's nice, but the reality is not anywhere near the ideal, I guess. But then, Guy No. 2 isn't perfect boyfriend material, either. He has a habit of only wanting what he can't have. I've seen him do this with other girls. And as tempted as I am to see where things go with him, I just feel as if he's going to lose interest as soon as he has me.

I keep going back and forth. I try to "listen to my heart," but it seems pretty mum at the moment. I'm torn, and although it was fine to see the two of them casually for a little while, I can tell they are both getting frustrated. Which guy do you think I should go for?

—Juggling

DEAR JUGGLING: Neither. Your heart is telling you that you don't really like either of these guys all that much. Don't have a boyfriend just for the sake of having a boyfriend. Keep your eyes, heart and calendar open for someone whom you'll choose without question.

Forever Single

DEAR ANNIE: I've wanted to write to you for a long time. I want to tell you my story. I am a 52-year-old man. I have never married and have never even been in a serious relationship. In my late teens, I was put in the position of being caretaker to two family members who were unable to take care of themselves.

When I was in my 20s, I made two attempts at looking for love, and both times ended with my getting hurt very badly. After that, I realized I had too much baggage to ever appeal to a woman, so I stopped looking and settled in to my role as family caretaker. The years—and the decades—went by.

About four years ago, both family members whom I was caring for died within only a few months of each other, and I am alone. I have thought about looking for love again, but I don't even know how to go about it anymore.

So I am resigned to being alone for the rest of my life. I have been in and out of therapy over the years and been on and off antidepressants. Nothing has really helped. I have gotten involved with a couple of community groups over the years but haven't really made any close friends.

I guess I'm not really writing for advice; it's too late for that. I am writing to tell people to try not to be so judgmental about the socially incompetent guy over there who often keeps to himself. You don't know his story, and he might be really nice if you took the time to get to know him.

—*Lonesome*

DEAR LONESOME: I am so sorry for the loss of your loved ones. Bless you for taking care of them for so long. I'm sure they appreciated it. But the fact is that it's not too late for advice unless you want it to be. So I'm giving you some anyway.

You are only 52 years old. You still have decades of life that can be full of love if you so choose. Don't look for someone to blame for your current state. Instead, focus on the present and what you can do now. Sign up for online dating sites, and don't let the sting of one rejection—or even 10—paralyze you. There is a woman who will love the way you're "different."

Need a Boyfriend With a Backbone

DEAR ANNIE: I am dating Jacob, a man I met online two years ago. Soon after we connected online, I broke it off with the guy I had been seeing and flew to meet Jacob in Utah, where he lives. We hit it off and decided to start a long-distance relationship. (I live on the East Coast.)

Things were great for the first few months. Then we started

176

fighting almost every day, mostly about small stuff; he wasn't calling me enough and hadn't visited me (when I had visited him twice). We worked out a better routine, and he started visiting me every few months. But now I'm dealing with some other issues.

Jacob is Mormon. (I'm not religious.) He isn't fully committed to his faith anymore, but he still goes to church every week and has a lot of friends from that community. One of these friends is a woman who is about his age (he's 40) and has taken to sending me threatening Facebook messages about how I am "bad" and Jacob is a "good man" who deserves "a nice Mormon girl." She makes me feel like a terrible person, and I've never even met this lady!

I brought this up with Jacob, but he continues to act as if everything is fine when he sees this woman in group settings. He said he doesn't want to confront her, because they have so many friends in common. I wish he would tell her to stop. He just laughs it off and says, "That's just how Mary is. Don't worry about her." Well, I do worry!

—*Secular Girlfriend*

DEAR SECULAR: Mormon or not, Jacob should not be allowing anyone to harass you in any way. If he is allowing this to go on from across the country, I shudder to think what he would tolerate if you lived in the same city. It sounds as if he either does not have much of a backbone to stick up for you or he does not care enough to. Move on and try to find a new boyfriend.

Ended for the Wrong Reason

DEAR ANNIE: I need your help with something. I am still in high school and have hit a bump in the road with a relationship issue.

I was dating this guy, "Andrew," for 10 months, and I really thought we had something going. Then I met this guy "Will," but we were just friends. One of my really good friends, "Natasha," would always talk to Andrew at the time, and it bothered me. I asked both of them whether anything was going on, and they both said no.

Later, I found out that Will liked me, but I didn't like him back. So Natasha and Will made up a plan to break Andrew and me up. They told lies about me, and Andrew believed them and broke up with me.

Now my used-to-be-friend Natasha and Andrew are dating, and though I am happy in the relationship that I am in now, I still feel hung up on him, and I am not quite sure how to get over him. He was a big part of my life, and my parents even approved of him. We talk every once in a while, and he seems happy where he is, but I am still wondering whether there will ever be a chance of our getting back together.

—Still Hung Up

DEAR STILL: Things ended abruptly and bizarrely, and now you're wondering what might have been. That's totally understandable.

But Andrew began disrespecting your relationship the minute he took Will and Natasha's word over yours, and he really fouled things up once he started dating Natasha. Just as any real friend wouldn't date your ex-boyfriend (without permission), any guy worthy of your love wouldn't immediately start dating your friend, no matter the circumstances.

Dating other people can be helpful after a breakup, as it's good to see for yourself that there are plenty more fish in the sea. But real closure can only come from within. If you're not smitten with your current boyfriend, don't hesitate to end things. You'll find someone who makes you forget all about Andrew eventually. In the meantime, focus on your own hobbies and goals, and spend quality time with true friends (i.e., not Natasha).

Wanting the Clothes-Free Life

DEAR ANNIE: I'm a man in my 30s who is a nudist at heart. Though I enjoy doing things clothes-free, my wife, "Jamie," does not. Jamie has gone with me to a nude beach—and "participated"—only once, and that was as a gift for my quitting smoking.

Jamie reluctantly allows me to attend one nudist event a year, but I have found myself wanting to do more—doing online research about different nudist sites in my area.

I know that Jamie would not want to go to any nudist events herself—though I would love it if she changed her mind—so I'm trying to figure out how best to broach the topic of my wanting to go alone.

The problem is that she, like so many others, mistakenly believes that naturism is a sexual thing. For me and the vast majority of nudists, it's not. I simply enjoy the freedom of being able to be outside naked. Also, most nudists are quite a bit older than I am.

How should I let my wife know about my desire to go to more nudist events?

—*Free Bird*

DEAR FREE BIRD: If being a naturist is that important to you, I would say to continue this dialogue with your wife about why you enjoy it and what the benefits are for you as an individual. Marriage is about compromise and seeing things from the other perspective, so it does put a small damper on just how free of a bird you can be.

Continue to talk to her about the importance of it to you, and be grateful that she does not object to your annual nudist event, especially because she has no interest in participating. You can never force someone to do something she does not want to do, but you can continue to communicate to her about why it is so important to you.

Phantom Lovers

DEAR ANNIE: It's been over a year now since my wife left for the fourth time. This time, I really don't have confirmation of her exact reason, but I can hazard a good guess, because the other three times she left for the same reason. She thinks I'm a cheater. In her mind, there is always someone else—but that's the only place there is someone else. I've never cheated.

I can't help but feel as if I'm free at last. I truly loved her and adored her. But I just couldn't take the mistrust any longer. For 13 years, I had my wallet dug through, Facebook account examined and email checked. I've been followed by numerous detectives. I know of two because I caught them, and my wife admitted she'd hired them. Here I was paying off bills so we could have a fun retirement, and she was paying detectives $500 a day to follow me. One time, at my work, one of my employees came to me visibly shaking. When I asked her what was wrong, she said, "Your wife offered me $100 to listen in on your phone calls, and, sir, I want nothing to do with this."

Annie, I could go on and on with the examples of mistrust. But for my own sanity, I had to move on. I kept saying to myself that the mistrust would pass, but it just never did. I've moved on, and now I'm with God. My question to you to finally put this to rest in my mind is: Is this some kind of illness?

—Free at Last

Dear Free at Last: Yes, it sounds as if she suffers from mental health issues that can only be addressed through professional treatment. I sincerely hope she gets the help she needs. It would be nearly impossible to get back together and stay together otherwise. Trying to build a marriage without trust is like trying to build a brick house without mortar. It cannot stand.

Jealousy Creeping In

DEAR ANNIE: I've never felt so strongly about anyone as I do about my girlfriend, "Angelina." She is warm and funny and makes me want to be my best self every day. The year that we've been dating has been the best of my life.

This is a great change from my previous girlfriend, who was from a well-to-do family and wasn't afraid to flaunt it. She was gorgeous but expected me to worship the ground she walked on because of that. She didn't like spending time with any of my friends. When she told me we couldn't go to my best friend's birthday party—because he's an "idiot," according to her—I decided to end it.

So it's no surprise that I'm thrilled Angelina clicks with my friends. She gets along so well with them, and they all think she's hilarious. I like going out with her and all my buds. I'm proud to show off what an awesome girlfriend I have.

The problem is that I feel she's getting along too well with some of them. I trust her (and them) completely and know I don't have to worry about infidelity. But I can't help but feel a little jealous when, for example, I realize my friends texted her about plans instead of me. When I've "jokingly" brought that up to her, she said it's because I'm bad about texting/calling people back and all my friends know it.

Another example: Recently, I was out of town for work for two weeks, and Angelina went out with my friends a few times. Sometimes I worry that she'll end up connecting better with one of my friends than with me. She and my best friend do click really well. As much as I don't want to be jealous, I feel that green monster sneaking up on me. Should I talk to her and/or my friends, or would I seem crazy?

—Love-Struck

DEAR LOVE: Your girlfriend loves your friends because she loves you, not the other way around—and don't you forget it. So often, jealousy is a self-fulfilling prophecy. Every time you indulge such a whim (telling your partner not to spend time with a certain person, asking for validation, etc.), you end up feeling even less secure and more in need of validation. Use positive self-talk ("My wonderful girlfriend loves me," "I love that my girlfriend cares about my friends," "What concrete facts are before me?") rather than positively talking yourself out of a happy relationship. It seems you've found a keeper, and I see no reason to goof things up by letting your insecurity call the shots.

Stopped Looking, Respectfully

DEAR ANNIE: In light of all the revelations about sexual misconduct by men toward women, I would like to share my personal experience. I am in my 60s and single and have never been married. I tried very hard for many years to find a woman I could go through life with but quit trying many years ago.

I have always been extremely respectful toward women and treated them with kindness and dignity. This, even when I was stood up for a date or had very mean and ugly remarks made to me. I have never been what I consider to be good at flirting, but that is mainly because I don't want to be disrespectful in any way.

I guess the main frustration for me has been the way that some friends and others I have observed have treated women in a very disrespectful manner but nonetheless have been able to have success wooing women. Of course, in many cases, these relationships haven't worked out, but I have always been somewhat amazed when women initially find a man's disrespectful behavior acceptable.

I realize and accept the fact that I will end my life alone, but I do find solace in knowing that I have never done anything to be ashamed of in my pursuit of a partner. I only wish that there had been a woman who found my qualities desirable.

—Lonely but Proud

DEAR LONELY BUT PROUD: Truly respecting women means respecting their intelligence and judgment. So rather than blame your loneliness on their taste in men, consider that something is lacking in your approach to dating. Perhaps you could improve your conversation skills or work on your confidence. When you feel good about yourself, other things fall into place. The inner critic pipes down; you can actually be present in real conversation and figure out whether you like someone (instead of just worrying about whether she likes you). This kind of genuine self-assuredness is palpable and magnetic to the right kind of partner.

You're only in your 60s. If you want to experience the joys of romantic partnership, I encourage you to adjust your technique and give love another shot. With all the online dating platforms, it's never been easier to find someone looking for the same things you are.

Tales From a Serial Monogamist

DEAR ANNIE: I can't seem to catch a break when it comes to my love life. I'm a serial monogamist; I began dating at 18, and I haven't spent so much as a month single since. But it seems as if just about every guy I've dated ends up being a cheater or a deadbeat.

Prior to my current relationship, I was with "Ray," who was underemployed. I had just received an inheritance (he didn't know about that when we started dating), so I had no problem being generous—at first. Gradually, I found myself paying for all his expenses. He didn't have a car, so I let him use mine. He never filled up the tank. I started to find his laziness and lack of ambition unattractive. That's when I started spending time with "Derek," who is a chef at the restaurant where I work, in a different light. Long story short, I broke things off with Ray and started seeing Derek.

I thought things were going great. But a few weeks ago, I went to use my laptop and noticed he was still logged on to Facebook. In general, I try not to snoop, but I couldn't help it this time. I saw the most recent message, which was from a girl, and they'd been talking regularly for the previous two months—flirting, sending each other selfies. I confronted Derek, and he insisted that they're just friends.

I don't really believe him, but I can't bring myself to leave him. I don't know whether there's anyone better out there. What is it with guys today?

—Serially Disappointed

DEAR SERIAL: You're jumping from relationship to relationship as a kid hops between couch cushions in a game of hot lava. What is so perilous about being single that you rush into shoddy relationships with men you don't much care for? That's not just a rhetorical question. I mean for you to really look inward and do some reflecting.

Instead of searching for your next boyfriend, you should be finding yourself. Break up with Derek. Don't date anyone for six months. Until you learn how to be happy with yourself, you won't be happy with a partner.

Affairs Revealed

DEAR ANNIE: My wife and I were married for 61 years. We had three sons. "Mary" passed away this year from complications of Parkinson's and dementia.

Mary and her friend "John" had a relationship most of our married life. She had gone to school with John and renewed their "friendship" soon after we were married in the 1950s. I only discovered all this about 10 years ago by finding John's name on telephone calls he'd made to our home. I could not act on it then because my wife was having cognitive impairment, which soon developed into dementia.

In the past, I had thought something was wrong with our marriage and asked my wife several times whether she wanted out, but she just said no. Maybe that was because in our generation, there was a stigma around getting divorced, or it could be that John's wife refused to give him a divorce.

It has devastated me, as I always thought my wife loved me. Evidently, she loved another man. Therapy did not help; I tried that. I cannot describe the hurt. My sons and their families do not know anything about this, and I cannot tell them, as they all loved my wife.

—*Sleepless in Anywhere, USA*

DEAR SLEEPLESS: I can't imagine what you're going through. My heart goes out to you. You're right not to tell your sons about their mother's affair, as that would benefit no one. Time is the only thing that will ease your pain.

And it might offer you some comfort to know you're not alone. Just this week, I received the following letter:

DEAR ANNIE: My wife of 59 years passed away three weeks ago. While going through her things after her death, I came across her diaries. She kept these her whole life. The worst mistake I have ever made in my life was to read these diaries.

I thought we had a very satisfying married life. We continued having sex well into our 70s. Thirty years ago, while I was away on a business trip, she and a friend went out barhopping. She met a guy whom she described as "a very caring and sexual man." She wrote, "He brought out feelings in me that I never thought I'd have." This man swept her off her feet, and she proceeded to have sex with him multiple times over the next month. She raved about how good the sex was.

During this time, we also had sex with each other at our usual frequency. At that time, she was 48 years old. She was beautiful. She could have passed for 28. She was an upstanding member of the community, was involved in various organizations and was a grandmother of two.

I cannot get over this affair. I cannot sleep or eat. I

keep visualizing what they were doing. This knowledge, on top of my grieving for her, is leaving me sick. There is no one I can talk to about this. I don't want the kids to know about it. I have always loved her deeply. In my heart, I have forgiven her.

Annie, what would make a woman who seemed otherwise stable and satisfied do something like that? What can I do to ease my pain? I cannot get this out of my mind.

—*Sick and Hurt*

DEAR SICK: I'm so sorry for your loss.

I don't know why your wife did what she did. Perhaps it was a midlife crisis and she wanted to feel desirable and young. But what she described in those pages was infatuation, not love. The terms might appear together in a thesaurus, but they have little to do with each other where it really counts.

Infatuation is intense, passionate and superficial. Love is patient, strong and selfless. It is the most profound kind of friendship. Infatuation fades with time; love only grows deeper. Infatuation's got nothing on love. Those few weeks several decades ago cannot negate the lifetime of happiness you shared. May your wife rest in peace. I wish you all the best.

Keep That Number Blocked

DEAR ANNIE: I used to date this guy, and I ended up

blocking his phone number. When we were seeing each other, he would only see me once every week or two. He only answered my messages or phone calls sometimes. We usually met late at night, and he would always make me leave his house early in the morning for some reason. I really miss him, and I think that we would really make each other happy if we were in a serious relationship. But he doesn't seem to be ready to open up with me or be serious with me. I slept with some other people while we were seeing each other, and I believe he was with other women then, too. He never does admit to it.

I believe that he has major feelings for me because I can feel our chemistry together. I know he sounds horrible, but I really think that he loves me. I have cried over him these past weeks, and I feel really sad that we are no longer talking. Should I continue moving on without him or try to pursue being with him if he ever does get in touch with me again? I will never call or message him again unless maybe he contacts me.

—*Curious for Advice*

DEAR CURIOUS FOR ADVICE: You blocked his number for a reason. It's time to block it again. I know you're looking for love and companionship, but you won't find it in him. Move on, even if you don't quite want to yet. Being single is so much better than being in a relationship with someone who doesn't appreciate you. Keep yourself open for someone who is thrilled to spend time with you. Don't give another day of your life to a man who only gives you his nights.

Long-Distance Love

DEAR ANNIE: I have been seeing this guy for a little over a year now. We met at a mutual friend's party while I was visiting New York. We had an instant connection. We were super attracted to each other and then found that we have a lot in common—the same sense of humor, same philosophies on life, same love of travel. It was immediately bittersweet, though, because he lives in New York City and I live in Los Angeles. We both felt that long-distance relationships never work, so we left our relationship as just friends, even though we both understood we were interested in more.

I travel to New York quite a bit and stay with him whenever I'm there. I always have a great time with him. I met up with him when I traveled to Asia, and we were inseparable.

Recently, I've been giving a lot of thought to getting serious with him, but there are a few other things aside from the distance holding me back. For one, he doesn't currently have a job even though he's been out of college for a few months. I worry he's unambitious. But I feel that if I don't give this a shot, I will always regret it. Should I give him a chance?

—Confused

DEAR CONFUSED: Contrary to popular cynical belief, long-distance relationships can work. In fact, according to my research, about 10 percent of marriages in the U.S. started out as long-distance relationships. The key is to have a light at the end of the tunnel. Doing the bicoastal thing with no end in sight makes it harder to cope, and it also makes you miss out on the real world outside your computer screen. You can't spend every Saturday night on Skype.

His unemployment is actually a plus here. There's no job

tying him to New York. Talk to him about working toward a future together in Los Angeles. Your chemistry sounds right, and now is the perfect time to test it out.

Where's the Beef?

DEAR ANNIE: I'm a self-proclaimed meatatarian. I suppose I eat vegetables from time to time, such as the lettuce and tomato on a hamburger. But for the most part, if it didn't have a central nervous system, I'm not interested.

You can't fault me for it; I grew up in the Midwest, where we treated sausage like a food group. I feel manly when I eat chicken wings, ripping flesh off the carcass of an animal with my teeth. Beef, chicken, duck, lamb, rabbit, bison, fish—love 'em all. However, I also love my new vegan (gasp) girlfriend.

Vegan Girlfriend is the best, and I've never felt this way before. She seems to really accept and love all of my personality. She's even fine with the meatatarian thing, never making any comments about it and saying it doesn't bother her.

My family really likes her, although it's always a process trying to explain her diet to Grandma, God bless her. ("No steak for her, Grandma. ... No, 'those people' don't eat chicken, either.")

I'm really starting to believe that Vegan Girlfriend is the one. But it keeps nagging at my mind that she's a vegan for a reason. Part of me thinks that underneath all her I-don't-minds, she is saying to herself, "How could you stuff another defenseless animal down your gullet when there is perfectly good kale in the fridge?"

I love this woman, but I also love meat. Am I doomed to a life of guilty animal consumption?

—*Meaty Mike*

DEAR MEATY: What's eating you? Your girlfriend doesn't care that you're an omnivore. She has said—and I quote—"I don't mind." You're projecting. On some level, you must feel bad about eating meat. Maybe that's your conscience nagging at you, or maybe it's just your cholesterol. Either way, figure it out and get right with it. And it wouldn't kill you to eat some of that perfectly good kale in the fridge.

Louse of a Partner

DEAR ANNIE: I am 44 years old and have been dating a 48-year-old man for 2 1/2 years. I met him three weeks after he got out of a 16-year relationship. There are some things I need help with. For most of the time we have been together, he has been talking to other women—sometimes his ex-girlfriend—on Facebook. He has told these other women that he loves them and misses them; he sends them heart and kissing emoticons. He "likes" their pictures on Facebook and leaves comments—for example, "Looking good!"—along with heart emojis. The thing is that he barely ever says these things to me.

I see him only on weekends, and we have takeout and watch

a movie. He barely ever holds my hand, and our sex life has all but stopped. He says he's too tired. He makes me feel as if I am the one in the wrong. He thinks it's perfectly acceptable to talk to all these women when he says about four words to me a day. He holds actual conversations with others. I can't tell you how many times I have fallen asleep beside him crying, and either he doesn't notice or he doesn't care.

I just can't handle this anymore. Should I just let him go and move on? If I did, I would most likely be alone. I am an amputee with not a lot of friends. I love him with all my heart, but I am tired of being walked all over. What should I do?

—*Confused in Small Town in Pennsylvania*

Dear Confused: You know exactly what you should do. But before we address the issue of leaving this louse, I want to encourage you to work on your self-esteem and make friends. Get involved in your community. Check Meetup, a website that connects people through shared interests, to see what clubs are in your town, or even start your own!

Now, back to the louse. This man does not deserve the love and affection you've given him. I promise you that it feels much better to be single than to be with someone who doesn't love you back. With time, you will find another mate. And do not sell yourself short in that regard. There is someone out there who will make you fall asleep smiling instead of crying.

Whether to Move In Together

DEAR ANNIE: All the advice columns I've read recommend not moving in together before marriage—or at least not before you and your partner have been dating for a year. I get the logic behind that, but in real life, things rarely follow a perfect timeline.

In my case, my boyfriend of six months, "Michael," has to move out of his house because his landlord is selling it. He has two months to find another place. We think it makes the most sense for him to move in with me. My apartment is plenty big. We'd both save money. We get along great and spend so much time together as it is.

Sure, I always thought I would wait a year before moving in with someone, too. But Michael and I have a great thing going. We have off-the-charts romantic chemistry, and we're very compatible as friends. We've never even had a fight.

We have discussed our living styles and think we would make good roommates. We're both in our mid-20s. What do you think? And please, with all due respect, I don't want to hear that "why buy the cow" line. I'm not writing to you for a lecture on marriage.

—Roommates-to-Be

DEAR ROOMMATES: Imagine a house that has no foundation but just sits atop the dirt. It may have been carefully constructed, with sturdy wooden walls and a dazzling slate roof. But when a hurricane blows through and there's nothing keeping the whole thing grounded, how long do you think that house will last?

No matter how great your chemistry with Michael, you don't deeply know each other. No matter how sunny things are now, storms will appear on the horizon eventually. (By the way, I wouldn't be so proud about never having had a fight. It's healthy to have conflicts in close relationships. It means you're both expressing yourselves.)

Convenience is not a good enough reason to move in together. Move in together when it's because it's the step you want to take in your relationship. You will never regret waiting; you'll very likely regret not waiting.

Nervous Empty Nester

DEAR ANNIE: Our 20-year-old son, "Harry," got his girlfriend pregnant, and he moved out last July. The baby was born in September. My wife, "Laura," is having a really hard time adjusting to his being out of the house. To make things worse, the girlfriend does not care for Laura. The relationship between them has been quite rocky. Harry works nights at the same place I do. Laura talks to him before he gets to work; we take him to dinner at his dinner break every night; and she talks to him on his way home from work, from 2:30 a.m. until 4 a.m.

Laura worries about seeing Harry all the time. It consumes her life. She posts stuff on Facebook about anxiety and suicide. She does have anxiety problems. Should I persuade her to go talk to someone, or is this a normal way for a mother to act when her firstborn moves out? She used to cry all the time, but that has stopped. Please help.

—*Worried Father and Husband*

DEAR WORRIED: Most parents do go through a period of sadness or anxiety when their children move out. But it sounds as if your wife is suffering from more than just empty-nest syndrome and instead has some deeper anxiety issues, for which your son is simply the current outlet. Her obsessiveness is interfering with her normal life, which means it's time to seek professional help.

Beyond that, I would also encourage you to take the initiative to do more things with just her. Take a vacation; go out on date nights; order pizza and watch a movie at home. In other words, show her some of the advantages to having the kids out of the house.

Propose to a Cheater?

DEAR ANNIE: I have been dating a wonderful woman and have been intending to ask her to marry me. We've made plans for the future together, but at present, I'm recovering from a horrible motorcycle accident. I won't be at 100 percent for a few months. I asked her whether that would be a problem, and she said no.

Well, it came to my attention that she has been sleeping around with three guys, one of whom is a nurse who cares for me. Needless to say, I was devastated—not only because I spent $13,000 on a ring and building a tiny home for us but because of the lies, deceit and unfaithfulness. I am an educated man with a successful business, and I know the smart thing to do would be to walk away. But I just can't let go.

—*All Twisted in Vermont*

DEAR TWISTED: You dodged a bullet, friend, and now you'd better stay clear of the line of fire. This woman cheated on you when you were down and out and needed love the most. You must be a sweet, forgiving person to describe her as "wonderful," and it was probably this sweetness that attracted her to you, like a shark to blood.

You need to get out of her range. End things, and then create as much distance as possible. Return or sell the ring, and use the cash for a vacation. Your heart needs a safe space to hide out and heal.

Seeking Relationship Closure

DEAR ANNIE: I feel like a cliché. About a year and a half ago, after six years of dating, "Jon" and I broke up—or more accurately, Jon broke up with me.

It blindsided me, especially because I had just relocated with him to another state about a month earlier. He said he was having personal issues and just wanted to be alone. He was drinking a lot and seemed really depressed at the time. I tried encouraging him to seek professional help, but he refused. I continued calling him periodically at first to check in and see whether he was doing OK. But I wanted to respect his wishes, and he didn't seem interested in getting back together, so I slowly began the process of healing and moving on.

About six months later, I started hearing from him again. He sent me gifts in the mail, references to inside jokes we'd shared over the years. He began calling a lot. I kept meaning to call him back, but for some reason, I didn't. Things were just different. I had started developing feelings for someone else. Eventually, Jon seemed to get this and began moving on, too. But I never could have guessed how quickly he'd move on.

He started seeing a woman he'd met on a dating site, and within three months, they were engaged. Their wedding is next month. And as much as I'm happy—I'm in a new relationship myself—I still sometimes dwell on how things ended with my ex. And I don't get how he never proposed to me after six years but it took him only three months to pop the question to a woman who was practically a stranger. I know it's silly, but I even have thoughts like, "Was I so horrible that anyone who came after me seemed like immediate marriage material?" And I feel this sense of unfinished business because I never did tell him how much he hurt me. I don't think he knows, because he invited me to the wedding. (I respectfully declined.) Do you think that calling him or writing him a letter just to have one final conversation would give me some sense of closure?

—*Conflicted*

DEAR CONFLICTED: Perhaps the cheapest form of therapy is putting thoughts down on paper. So write Jon a letter, but don't send it. Instead, use it as a space to work out your feelings and figure out what's really stopping you from moving on. Closure is a gift we can only give to ourselves.

Sexless Marriage

DEAR ANNIE: My husband and I have been married for over 30 years. In many ways, we are very compatible and have shared interests in music, books and movies. However, we no longer have a sex life or any form of intimacy. It has been almost 10 years since he expressed an interest in being with me. He also refuses to discuss the issue.

In the past few years, whenever I try to talk about my unhappiness, he maintains that I am narcissistic and asks me not to nag him about it. I know he has performance problems, and it doesn't help that he drinks every night. He has also told me that although he loves me, he is not in love with me and considers us companions.

I have gone for counseling, but I feel as if I say the same things over and over with no resolution. I think my husband hopes I'll forget about sex and learn to be content with the situation. Because I am near retirement age and used to living with a family, the idea of living alone scares me, but I can't continue living in limbo.

—Sad and Fed Up

DEAR SAD: Your concerns don't make you a narcissist; they make you normal. Ten years is not part of the normal intimacy ebb-and-flow all couples experience. A fulfilling sex life is part of any healthy marriage—and so is communication. Your husband is shutting you down on both fronts. Rather than talk about the problem, he blames you for even caring. He's using the tired old defense mechanism called deflection. Don't fall for it.

It sounds as if your husband is suffering from depression. Tell him that whether he wants to recognize that there is a problem or not, his refusal to get help is hurting you. Implore him to seek counseling. It also may be that he is an alcoholic. At the very least, his drinking bothers you. That's reason enough for you to attend an Al-Anon meeting (by yourself), where you will find a roomful of people who can relate to what you're going through. I wish you all the best.

Leap of Faith

DEAR ANNIE: Last year, I got out of a 10-year relationship. I thought she was the love of my life—until she cheated on me with one of my friends. I was devastated, and only recently have I started to be remotely interested in dating again. Lately, I've been on a few dates with this girl—let's call her "Lauren"—and she is amazing. She's so beautiful and talented and kind. Just being around her makes me feel like a better person. I want to take things to the next level, but there's something holding me back.

I'm not sure I can bring myself to trust someone with my emotions ever again. What's the point of making ourselves so vulnerable when it so often just ends in heartache? This girl has set off no red flags, yet I keep waiting for the other shoe to drop. How do people ever move on after such dramatic breakups?

—In My Shell

DEAR SHELL: Risk is what makes trust possible. It's the gap that lets us take a leap of faith. If there weren't the possibility of falling, the feeling of landing safely on the other side would mean very little.

That's not to say we should jump into relationships recklessly or walk through life blindfolded. It's only natural—healthy, even—for you to feel cautious after what your ex-girlfriend did. But this new woman has given every indication that she is worthy of your trust. Go for it.

Sleep Tight

DEAR ANNIE: My husband and I have been having an ongoing conflict about when to go to bed at night, as he insists we go to bed at the same time. I am more of a night owl and sometimes will want to stay up until around 11, either because I'm not tired yet or because I want to watch a movie or program that's not over until then.

My husband wants us to go to bed at 10, stating that it's the only way to get enough sleep because our dog consistently wakes us up around 6. He says that when I go to bed after him, I wake him up while crawling into bed, causing him not to be able to fall asleep again for hours. Also, he routinely falls asleep while watching TV in the living room and says that if he's not woken by 10 to come to bed, he can't get back to sleep. I do think that sometimes the reason he can't get back to sleep is that he's allowed himself to get worked up over the fact that I didn't wake him at 10 as instructed.

This bedtime issue has caused huge fights. He accuses me of being selfish and not caring about the impact the lack of sleep will have on his health, while I feel that he's being controlling and treating me like a child by forcing me to go to bed at a certain time. I believe that he's sincere about his sleep issues and that his point is not to control me, but I never imagined that as an adult I'd have an imposed bedtime.

I think there are larger issues at play. If I consistently acquiesce to his desired bedtime, will I be allowing him to treat me like a child, or will I, as he argues, be making a wise adult decision to do what's best for our marriage and health? Each of us thinks the other is being unreasonable, and at this point, I am confused and don't know who's right. But I do know I missed the end of the most exciting World Series in years.

—Tired of the Fight

DEAR TIRED: Shame on him for denying you the chance to witness that breathtaking 10th inning. Even children should have been allowed to break their bedtimes for that one. Speaking of children: Don't let your husband treat you like one. It sounds as if he has a bit of a controlling streak, and it will only grow bigger if you take his demands lying down. So be firm—but also compromise. Perhaps that means agreeing to go to bed at the same time once or twice a week.

To address the issue of your waking him up when you get in bed, consider getting two twin beds and pushing them together. I've heard from many readers that this works well.

Snooping and Trust

DEAR ANNIE: Why do women think it's OK to snoop

through boyfriends' phones or social media? It's such an invasion of privacy.

For background: I'm a guy in my late 20s. I'm trustworthy (I think). I've never cheated on a girlfriend. Yet a few women I've dated over the past few years have snooped. One read my emails when I left myself logged in on her computer. (I found out because a few emails were mysteriously already marked as read. Not great at covering her tracks.) The other didn't exactly snoop, but I noticed when she was showing me something on her phone that she had been Googling my ex-girlfriend's name. I took both those things as red flags. I want to date someone who is secure enough not to be jealous or suspicious.

I was talking to a group of my female friends about this, and all except one admitted that they've snooped, too. Most said they know it's bad, but one girl defended it: "If he's got nothing to hide, what's the big deal? And if he is messing around, I'd rather know so I can move on." Isn't that sad?

I guess I'm just venting at this point, but I would love to hear your take on this one.

—*Disappointed Dude*

DEAR DISAPPOINTED: My take is the same as yours. Trust is the foundation of a good relationship. If you feel that you can't trust your partner, to the point that you'll invade his or her privacy, then what's the point? There is no love without trust. Have faith in your relationship, and it will flourish or not, but at least you'll have given yourself wholly to it. I hope the next woman you date understands this.

The One Who Got Away?

DEAR ANNIE: My wife and I are in our late 50s and met in high school. "Barb" was the girl of my dreams, a cheerleader, popular and athletic. We began dating as seniors and married after I graduated from college. After we married, I noticed that Barb had little interest in sex. I was always the initiator, and this seemed to irritate her and made our intimacy rare. I decided to bury myself in my work and ignored the issue.

Today, we are happily married and have children and grandchildren, and she is still my best friend. Sex isn't as much an issue, as I am older and have ignored my sexuality for years anyway.

While we were dating back when, there was another girl, "Helen," who made it obvious that she was interested in me. Helen was easily the prettiest girl I had ever met, but I ignored those feelings and stayed true to Barb. I would see Helen at reunions—the five-year, 10-year and 15-year—and it took me a few months each time to get over the feelings that I had for her. We stopped going to these reunions, partly because we had moved to another state and it was inconvenient to travel.

The most recent reunion was arranged over social media, and I kept seeing pictures of Helen. She is still gorgeous, married with children and grandchildren. Three years later, I am still compelled to Google her to learn everything I can about her. This has turned into a compulsion that I cannot stop. I haven't told my wife because this would only create havoc in our marriage. I am not interested in speaking to a psychologist. My question is simple. How many people suffer from such feelings—feelings that they may have made a mistake but must now live with it to save the feelings of another?

—*Love Lost*

DEAR LOVE LOST: I'm sure many people at some point indulge in a bit of "what if" daydreaming, whether it be about another person they might have married or a career path they might have taken. But we all know that the grass isn't really greener on the other side; it just seems that way to those unsatisfied with their lot. Your crush on Helen has more to do with your relationship with Barb. The fact that you've ignored your sexuality for years doesn't mean it's not an issue anymore. Though every marriage is different, it's important to share some form of intimacy. Redirect the energy spent Googling Helen into searching for ways to revitalize your marriage, whether through counseling or an open, noncritical conversation with Barb.

Acting for the Right Reasons?

DEAR ANNIE: I moved from the city to the country about 20 years ago, and now that my husband is deceased, I plan to return to an urban environment. I have spent many hours researching different locations, including using the internet and driving through neighborhoods, and I believe I've found a centrally located area that is upscale but affordable. Basically, almost everything I'm looking for is at this location.

The problem is that in the past year, I have been dating a guy who also lives in that area. I am in love with him, and I've told him so—even though I'm sure I will never hear those words from him, simply because of his nature. But he calls me every night, and we see each other once a week, so I know that he is fond of me. The reason I told him I love him is that over the past few months, he has developed an illness that is going to result in a rather complicated surgery. I felt that he should know how I feel, and I knew I would regret not having told him if something should happen. I am 65, and he is 70.

Truthfully, I could search around a different city and find a similar location with the same amenities. I am not religious, and I am very conscious of the limited time that we both have here on this earth. How do I know whether I'm moving there for him or I'm moving there for me?

—*Moving Motivations*

DEAR MOVING: You don't need a polygraph to figure out whether you're lying to yourself. You just need your heart and a willingness to listen to it. So take this two-question test.

1) Would you still move to this town if this man didn't live there? 2) How would you feel if you two broke up six months from now—committed to building a life on your own in your new town or inclined to pack up and move elsewhere?

Be deeply honest in this self-evaluation and you'll make the decision that's right for you. Fudge the answers and you'll only be cheating yourself.

The Thrill Is Gone

DEAR ANNIE: I have been married to the same man for 59 years. I have one daughter and am an immigrant to this country. I think I am a fairly decent cook and housekeeper. I worked for 30 years in a very large company and ended my career in management. I read a lot; I play bridge. All in all, I am easy to get along with.

My husband is an intelligent man, though he is not a great talker. His interests are the stock market and making money. He has a few friends, but they're of the casual type. I would call him emotionally challenged. He comes from a very large family, and I get along with his family members very well. He cares for them and has helped them out.

This week, I celebrated a milestone birthday. There was no card, no flowers, nothing. When I remarked on it, he told me he had been planning to buy me a card and give me an airline ticket for a trip that we decided on six months ago and is coming up in a month. I told him I don't think it qualifies as a gift. Even after a lengthy discussion, he didn't change his mind.

I should add that he has not bought me a birthday card or a gift for the past 20 years.

My feeling is that his sole interest in me is as a provider of meals, as a housekeeper and as a contributor of money.

When I retired, I had a very substantial fund, which he invested himself. For a few years, it did very well. Then he went behind my back and made a risky investment. We lost our house, and things were dire for a few years.

My feeling is that he has a problem dealing with women. He never abides by my opinion on any topic. He is not particularly warm toward any female in the family, and my daughter sometimes calls him an iceberg.

What makes this man tick? I am getting to the point where I don't think I can stand him anymore. However, I am too old to leave. Any advice would be appreciated.

—*Fed Up to the Teeth*

DEAR FED: You deserve better, and if your husband won't deliver that, go get it for yourself. No, I am not prescribing an affair. What I mean is that you should stop focusing so much on what makes your husband tick and focus instead on what makes you tick. Cultivate your hobbies. Plan outings with your daughter or your friends. Have dinner with your favorite in-laws. Go see a new movie. Curl up with a big stack of good books. In short, celebrate yourself.

You sound like a friendly, kind and independent woman. Whether or not your husband realizes it, he's a very lucky man.

Close Colleague

DEAR ANNIE: A woman recently started to get close with my husband at work. She always finds excuses to ask him to do things with her alone. From what I heard before meeting her, she sounded smart and fun. My husband said that she often asked about me and said she wanted to meet me.

I know my husband and trust him. We love passionately. So I wasn't bothered by it at the beginning and was happy for him to have another friend at work. But when I invited her to our home with other friends, she always couldn't come for a funny reason.

Then one day, my husband and I ran into her on the street. I was excited to finally meet this amazing woman, but she barely talked to me, looked at me or used my name. She kept seeking eye contact with my husband, saying his name and walking next to him closely so that I had to be squeezed out from the middle and walk behind them. She acted as if she were the wife and I were the third person.

I like to see the good side of people, but I was not able to see that nice person my husband described to me at all. I found her behavior toward me rude and aggressive. If her only intention were to be a good friend of my husband's and she truly had wanted to meet me, she wouldn't have acted so hostilely. I think she is just manipulative. When I shared my thoughts with my husband, as expected, he didn't want to believe me. Instead, he said I am paranoid and jealous. Of course. She had succeeded in presenting this perfect image of herself to him. Now the more I say against her the more she'll be the innocent victim. It's a trick that all women know, but very few men are capable of understanding the complexity of women's nature.

I can't stand this disrespect, and I don't want my husband to be around a fake person. How can I get him to realize that she is not what he thinks? I look forward to reading your advice. It will be easier for my husband to get the message when it comes from an independent voice.

—*Frustrated*

DEAR FRUSTRATED: This lady has two faces, and neither one is pretty. With one, she is trying to manipulate a married man into believing she is a sweet pal; with the other, she's grimacing while all but elbowing his wife into the gutter. Trust your gut, and ask your husband to trust it, too.

Those Wandering Eyes

DEAR ANNIE: I just do not know the best way to handle this situation. I have been living happily with my partner for six years. He is kind and, for the most part, considerate. But the following scenario has been going on almost from the beginning.

Often when he notices a woman he finds attractive when we are in a restaurant or in a crowd, he does not take his eyes off her. He detaches himself from the conversation at hand and is obviously intrigued. Even if we are getting up to leave, he is gazing at her as he is doing up his coat.

Is it because he wants to be noticed by her? He claims not. But of course, it is inevitable that she does notice.

Each time he does this, I tell him I find it insulting and demeaning. And he says he'll try not to do it again. Is this something he cannot control? I try to swallow it, but instead I seethe inside.

—Distracted By His Distraction

DEAR DISTRACTED: Glancing at an attractive woman is OK and often hard to resist doing for a moment. Anything longer than that is leering, which is rude. And leering in front of one's girlfriend? "Sleazy" doesn't begin to cover it. It's downright disrespectful. While he's staring down some unwitting woman across the restaurant, you're sitting there not only ignored but also forced to watch the creep show.

The good news is that he is honest and has admitted he is doing it. To me, that says there is hope. It's time to have a very serious conversation about how this is impacting your relationship. If he truly cares, he'll work on breaking the habit. Whatever you do, stop swallowing your anger. It will burn you up inside.

Wanting to Break Free

DEAR ANNIE: I am a somewhat attractive, financially independent woman in her 50s, and I've been divorced for 27 years. I have been involved with the same man on and off for the past 12 years. We became involved while he was separated—or so I was informed. It took me a while to discover this was not totally accurate, and we stopped seeing each other until he obtained a divorce. His children hate me, even though I was not to blame for his choice.

He eventually cheated on me, and afterward I discovered that he had cheated several times during his 19-year marriage. I removed him from my life for quite some time but unfortunately let him back in after he claimed he was very much in love with me and did not want to be with anyone else. We went through counseling, and I thought we were moving forward, only to discover several months later he was chasing strippers. I was an even bigger idiot and still let him back in my life.

We do not spend holidays together, although I do see him weekly. We also work in the same town and are both well-known. I know he lies to his family, business clients and me so he can do whatever he wants. Though we had previously purchased a home together, he recently chose to purchase a different home in which to live. His ego and arrogance are insurmountable, yet I have been unable to let him go and remove him permanently from my life. I truly need to find a way to extricate myself and move forward so that I can live a life with someone who actually wants to be with me. What is wrong with me, and how do I break this vicious cycle, seeing as this is clearly my issue and not his?

—Weak and on Bended Knee

DEAR WEAK: First, be nicer to yourself. Calling yourself an idiot or weakling only contributes to low self-esteem, which is most likely why you're hung up on this lowlife in the first place.

You're smart; you've got a good handle on the situation and what you need to do. Sometimes the head needs to lead the way and the heart will follow. In other words, start pretending you're really over this man and, in time, you will be.

To do this, you must first make a clean break. If you still have any assets together, disentangle them, and then cut off all communication. When you find your hand hovering over the phone—dangerously close to his number—call a friend instead, or just go for a walk. It might seem overwhelming, but just take it one day at a time. I promise it will get easier. When he comes crawling back again—and he will—resist. You will feel infinitely stronger afterward.

Baby, Won't You Look My Way?

DEAR ANNIE: I am a 21-year-old guy in college. I am on my school's cross-country and track teams, and in my spare time, I am the bass guitarist and one of the vocalists for a band.

Here's the issue: Despite what appear to be ideal opportunities to meet women, none seems to be interested in me. I'm friends with several of them, but that's as good as it gets.

I guess it's because of my looks. I have a crooked nose; my ears stick out (I mean WAY out); I have a gap in my front teeth (like David Letterman); and I have freckles under my eyes. Think Alfred E. Neuman from Mad magazine but with brown hair instead of bright red.

I'm also very skinny, which I need to be to run miles in short periods of time. I know that some girls like guys with muscles, so that rules me out.

When the band gets done playing for the night, it's as if the room tilts away from me, as all the girls are talking to my better-looking band mates. The only girls who come talk to me are either relatives or those who ask me to introduce them to one of the other band members. (This happens frequently.)

I don't mean to make this some sort of misogynistic rant. I know that women can't control whom they are attracted to any more than my male friends and I can control whom we are attracted to.

I've thought about asking both male and female friends what my problem may be or what I could do to improve the situation, but I can't because I'm too embarrassed.

I'm an athlete AND a musician. I shouldn't have any problem at all, right? Please help.

—*Stuck Alone*

DEAR STUCK: Trust me, not all girls prefer human Ken dolls. The "imperfect" attributes you mentioned can add to your charm. You just have to learn how to make them work for you. You can do that using the single most attractive trait: confidence.

So be confident that exactly who you are is enough. Let your warmth and intelligence shine through. Crack jokes; laughter is an aphrodisiac. When you're playing shows, flash that gap-toothed grin proudly and women will think it's the cutest smile they've ever seen.

It may be a "fake it till you make it"-type process, but gradually you'll start to feel that room tilt in your direction.

Will You?

DEAR ANNIE: I never proposed marriage to my wife, and if you think it's worthy of printing, I will correct that in your column. We're both faithful readers, so I'm sure she'll see it. Here's our story.

My family moved to our city during Christmas break of the

fifth grade. Though my future wife and I lived within a mile of each other and could both walk to school, we had no classes together and never met. In junior high, we rode different school buses and shared no classes together. In high school, the 10th and 11th grades brought no classes together, and still we never crossed paths. Our senior year, in preparation of college, we both took typing. That's the one class we ever shared. We started dating. We spent the first two years of college apart, but when we were home, we dated and spent a small fortune on stamps and envelopes to stay in touch. We spent the last two years of college together at the same university, and we dated each other exclusively. On a trip home during that last two years, we went to a jewelry store and put matching wedding bands on layaway. There was no engagement ring, nor was there a proposal. We just knew we were going to marry. So, now I'd like to ask: Teresa, will you marry me—again?

—Bill

DEAR BILL: This is certainly a first, but your letter gave me such a smile I couldn't not print it. I hope she says yes.

◆

Ask Me Anything

216

Resources

AIDS Hotline
800-232-4636

American Chronic Pain Association
800-533-3231
https://theacpa.org

AA (Alcoholics Anonymous)
http://www.aa.org

Al-Anon (for families of alcoholics)
800-344-2666
http://www.al-anon.org

Center for Employment Opportunities
510-251-2240
https://ceoworks.org

Child Help USA National Child Abuse Hotline
800-422-4453

Eating Disorders Awareness and Prevention
800-931-2237
https://www.nationaleatingdisorders.org

GLBT National Help Center
888-843-4564
https://www.glbthotline.org/

Grief Recovery Institute
818-907-9600
https://www.griefrecoverymethod.com

Resources Cont.

Job Accommodation Network
800-ADA-WORK
https://askjan.org

Medicare
800-638-6833
https://www.medicare.gov/

Men of Valor Academy
510-567-1308
http://www.menofvaloracademy.org

NA (Narcotics Anonymous)
http://www.na.org

National Council on Alcoholism and Drug Dependence Hopeline
800-622-2255

National Council on Problem Gambling
800-522-4700
https://www.ncpgambling.org

The National Domestic Violence Hotline
800-799-7233

National Help Line for Substance Abuse
800-262-2463

National Hopeline Network
800-273-8255
http://www.mentalhealthamerica.net

Resources Cont.

National OCD Information Hotline
800-NEWS-4-OCD

National Youth Crisis Hotline
800-442-4673

Office for Civil Rights, U.S. Department of Education
800-872-5327
https://www2.ed.gov/about/offices/list/ocr/index.html

PsychINFO American Psychological Association
800-374-2722
http://www.apa.org/psycinfo

Rape, Abuse, and Incest National Network (RAINN)
800-656-HOPE
https://www.rainn.org

Social Security Administration
800-772-1213
https://www.ssa.gov
https://identitytheft.gov

Veterans Crisis Line (24/7)
800-273-8255 and press 1
https://www.veteranscrisisline.net
Send a text message to 83825

Special Acknowledgments

COURTNEY DAVISON grew up in Kimberton, Pennsylvania, and Virginia Beach, Virginia. She attended the Savannah College of Art and Design, where she received a scholarship for writing. In 2011, she won the Savannah Morning News Poetry Contest, judged by poet Patricia Lockwood. After completing her BFA in 2012, she moved to California for work and fell in love with the Golden State.

She has copyedited dozens of novels and nonfiction manuscripts as well as thousands of short-form pieces, including internationally syndicated columns, press releases and essays. Her writing has appeared in publications around the world.

She lives in Los Angeles, California, with her cat, Timber.

About the Author

ANNIE LANE grew up in California before heading east at the age of 18. She graduated with honors from New York University, where she majored in English literature and specialized in psychology. After NYU, she earned her Juris Doctor from New York Law School.

A lifelong learner, Annie has held a variety of jobs, including working in a law firm and for a federal magistrate. She is a certified yoga instructor with sales experience from an internet-advertising startup. Because of her great love for books and writing, Annie has also worked for Barnes & Noble and freelanced for various publications.

Since July 2016, Annie has been offering common-sense solutions to everyday problems in her internationally syndicated column, "DEAR ANNIE." Her advice is unusually perceptive. She is sympathetic, funny and firm—echoing the style of her biggest inspiration, Ann Landers.

Annie lives outside Manhattan with her husband, two kids and two dogs. When she is not writing, she devotes her time to play dates and Play-Doh.

ASK ME ANYTHING

is also available as an e-book for Kindle, Amazon Fire, iPad, Nook and Android e-readers. Visit creatorspublishing.com to learn more.

o o o

CREATORS PUBLISHING

We find compelling storytellers and

help them craft their narrative,

distributing their novels and collections

worldwide.

o o o